Scripturally saturated and super practical, *Walking Together* will lead readers to a richer understanding of authentic discipleship. Doering leads us to see that at its core, discipleship is fueled by the Gospel, rooted in Word and worship, and best lived out in community. You'll love the questions at the end of each chapter, that makes this a very group-friendly book. If you've been looking for a resource that helps you better follow Jesus, this is the road map for you!

Rev. Brian Davies, Lord of Glory Lutheran Church, author of
Connected to Christ: Overcoming Isolation through Community

Ted Doering invites the reader into a personal journey of discipleship by sharing his story and, more important, the story of the Gospel. By weaving together personal narrative, the truths of Scripture, and practical ideas for discipleship, Pastor Doering challenges readers to think how they will live their lives to love God and their neighbor. Get ready to go on an adventurous journey that will make a difference in your life and the lives of others.

Don Christian, president, Concordia University Texas

Profound but simple. Supernatural but ordinary. Eternal but everyday. This is the beautiful mystery revealed in *Walking Together*. Ted Doering shows that being a disciple who makes disciples is not a chore or achievement but a gift of God, lived in real time, propelled by His living Word. For anxious and isolated people, Doering opens up the biblical way of life that builds hearts, binds souls together, and blesses a lost world with God's life-transforming love.

Rev. Michael W. Newman, author of *Hope When Your Heart Breaks* and
Getting Through Grief: Eight Biblical Gifts for Living with Loss

Through storytelling and Scripture, *Walking Together* presents a refreshing look at the beauty and importance of discipleship. Ted Doering guides us to see the hope of the Gospel while encouraging us to live out the way of Jesus in community with others. After all, we were never meant to do this alone, but we were created to walk through this life together.

Tanner Olson, author, poet, speaker,
and founder of Writtentospeak.com

The mark of a good teacher is the ability to take a complex topic and make it understandable for the everyday person. With humor and relatable stories, Ted takes the intimidating topic of discipleship and makes accessible the process of trusting Jesus' promises and following Him. *Walking Together* marries deep theological truths with practical next steps. It's a great read for all who want to grow in their journey with Jesus and invite others along!

Mark T. Pulliam, pastor and church planter, Lazarus Church

"Go and make disciples" is a simple, yet intimidating, command. Where do we begin? In *Walking Together*, Ted invites readers to take one small step and then another as he takes discipleship from concept to action. If you treat this less like a textbook and more like a workbook, you will most certainly be changed by the time you reach the last page. Furthermore, if you follow his instruction to read the book with others, you will be living out the very lessons it holds. So find a few friends and, as the title suggests, walk together.

Laura Pulliam, DCE and church planter, Lazarus Church

In a time when discipleship has been promoted as a Law-based, individual endeavor, *Walking Together* provides a refreshing, biblical approach to discipleship as a journey we take together as the Body of Christ. Relying on Scripture and our Lutheran confession of the faith, Ted Doering offers an encouraging, practical pathway for disciples. It is insightful, helpful, and at times, challenging resource for any believer wanting to grow in discipleship.

Rev. Dr. Mark A. Wood is director of LCMS witness and outreach
ministry and the LCMS revitalization initiative

WALKING TOGETHER

SIMPLE STEPS FOR DISCIPLESHIP

Ted Doering

CONCORDIA PUBLISHING HOUSE · SAINT LOUIS

Published by Concordia Publishing House
3558 S. Jefferson Avenue, St. Louis, MO 63118-3968
1-800-325-3040 • cph.org

Manufactured in the United States of America

Library of Congress Cataloging-in-Publication Data

Names: Doering, Ted, author.
Title: Walking together : simple steps for discipleship / Ted Doering.
Description: Saint Louis, MO : Concordia Publishing House, [2021] | Summary: "The landscape of discipleship in the American Church consists of a vast array of different ideas, programs, and processes, many of which rely on works as a litmus test to measure people's faith. But discipleship looks different when it is founded on our identity in the Gospel and fueled by the good gifts God gives to us. This Lutheran sacramental outlook shows that discipleship is a simple but difficult process lived in the daily rhythms of life. Simply put, discipleship is trusting the promises of Jesus and seeking to follow Him. The author will lead readers on a journey to discover the rhythm of simple discipleship as they trust Christ's Word, seek God's wisdom, and follow His will"-- Provided by publisher.
Identifiers: LCCN 2021002856 (print) | LCCN 2021002857 (ebook) | ISBN 9780758669391 (paperback) | ISBN 9780758669407 (ebook)
Subjects: LCSH: Spiritual formation--Lutheran Church.
Classification: LCC BV4511 .D64 2021 (print) | LCC BV4511 (ebook) | DDC 248.4/841--dc23
LC record available at https://lccn.loc.gov/2021002856
LC ebook record available at https://lccn.loc.gov/2021002857

1 2 3 4 5 6 7 8 9 10   30 29 28 27 26 25 24 23 22 21

CONTENTS

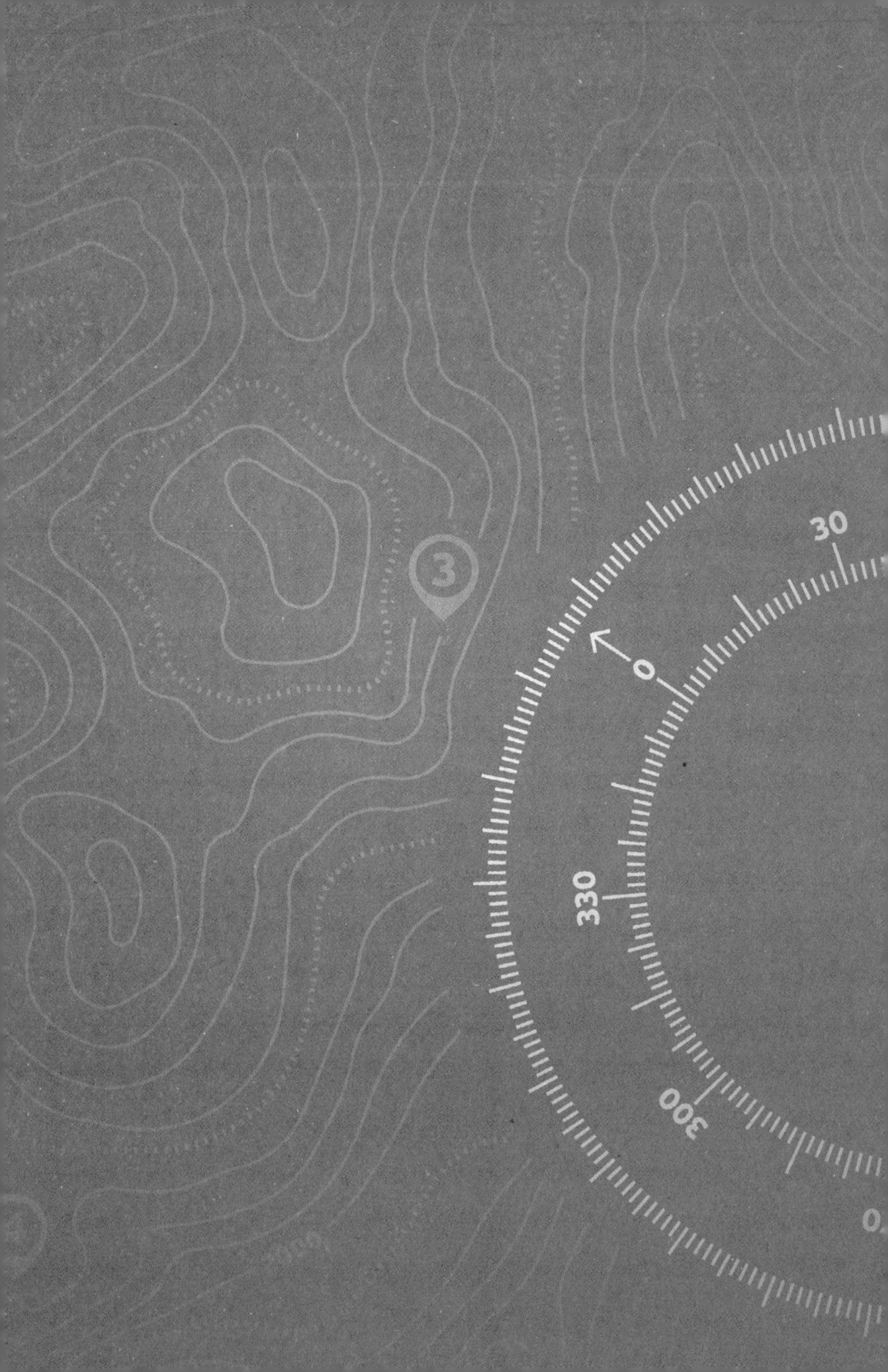
3
30
330
300
0

How to Use This Book

Discipleship is an interesting idea. In fact, in the Bible you won't find the word *discipleship* or the word *disciple* used as a verb. What you will find is that we are called to make disciples. As you'll read throughout this book and learn as you go, that task is not to be taken on alone.

This book is meant to be read in a group along with other people seeking to learn more about the discipleship journey. The book is broken down into the different aspects of discipleship: trusting, seeking, and following. A small devotion and thought will lead into each new section of chapters. At the end of every chapter is a section titled "Discipleship Community." This section will give you a chance not only to discuss but also to practice what you have learned. While you could do all of this on your own, I have found that it is much more beneficial to walk together with fellow brothers and sisters in Christ. They are there to check in and hold you accountable, to ask you what you are learning, and to point you back to Jesus. In Scripture, whenever we see people go off on their own to seek God, they always return to the group afterward. This is not a solitary pursuit. Find some folks to walk through this with you.

Discipleship is a lifelong pursuit. You may encounter this book at the start of that journey, or you may find it after many years of being a Christian. Either way, there is encouragement here for you. There is no answer key for the Discipleship Community questions and activities. The point is not that somewhere there is a formula that makes you a good disciple. You will read that Jesus makes you a disciple and that the rest is a gift from Him. You can bring your group together around coffee at your local shop or in the fellowship hall on a Sunday morning. Maybe you are reading this book together as a family around the kitchen table. These are all great options. If someone isn't already leading the group, designate a person to be the discussion leader. The leader's job is to keep the group on point and help push deeper into the discussion, not to have all the right answers. The goal here is to share what God is doing through His Word and work in your life. How do we know this works? "And they have conquered him by the blood of the Lamb and by the word of their testimony, for they loved not their lives even unto death" (Revelation 12:11). Your testimony shared together not only builds your own spiritual life but also builds up those around you.

While writing this book, I have been field-testing it with a group from my church. In spending time together on the discipleship journey, we have found some great ways to use our time together to discuss and grow. Discipleship should not happen alone. Working in a group brings the gift of the Body of Christ into the equation. Your group can use these tips as well.

- Discipleship is for both introverts and extroverts. Because the questions are included in the chapters, you will have a chance to see them beforehand, giving introverts time to think ahead and extroverts time to narrow down their answers. Talking about your faith can be daunting, but remember, it should be simple. Let introverts have the space to think and build up their answers. Extroverts, and I speak as one myself, can weigh through the process of when to speak and especially be quick to listen.

- Allow yourself and those you are reading with to be pushed into comfort, but out of your comfort zone. Let there be constant reminders of what Jesus has done and that your identity is found in your Baptism. Nothing can take that from you. Sin, however, will seek to make you comfortable. There will be a deeper discussion in this book about being *comforted* versus being *comfortable*. As you process this book in a group, remember that while you live in the comfort of Jesus' salvation for you, He has created you to do good works—the process of sanctification. Do not seek to simply read and remain where you are as a Christian. Instead, see where Jesus is working in your life. Leaders, try to walk this fine line. Use your wisdom to find times when you need to call people deeper and times when they just need to rest in the knowledge of Jesus.

- This time is not a therapy session. When Christians gather around the Word, there is temptation to try to fix one another. While there will be iron sharpening iron, this is not the time to ask people to share more than they are willing. The goal is not to fix people. Instead, the goal is to take one more step in discipleship. It is to trust, seek, and follow Jesus.

- Take notes. You have full permission to write all over this book—in the margins or in the midst of the text. Grab a highlighter. If you are an overachiever, grab your set of different-colored highlighters that each carry a specific meaning. Take time to write out the questions you have or the thoughts that are sparked. Grab a journal or take notes electronically. This is not because this book is overly stuffed with wisdom or is the authority on the subject. No, this is so that as you process what is going on in this book, you can see where God is calling you. We will discuss discipleship as a journey; a journal or notes will help you to see how far you have come. They will show you what has happened along the way.

- Read this book with your Bible open. Much of the Scripture used will be printed within these pages, but dive deeper. Look at the context surrounding the Scripture passage and how it plays to the chapter and book as a whole. It cannot be overstated how important the Bible is to the life of a disciple. Keep it with you as you read.

- Pray as you read. Some concepts may be old hat for you. But others may be challenging and may push you. Pray about them. Pray together with the people you are reading this book with. Bring your needs before God.

- Do it. Discipleship does not happen because you think really hard about it. It is not a theoretical, theological idea. It is about everyday life. As you read through this book, do it. Receive God's Word, step out in faith, and see how the Holy Spirit works in your life. The temptation with books like this one is to read it through, argue about what you like and don't like, then move on to the next. Each chapter will give you a chance to put into practice what you have learned. Don't let those ideas sit on the page. Put them into practice and watch how God will work.

- Take your time. This book can be read over several weeks as a short-term study for your group, but my encouragement is to spend a year together, meeting either once a week or every other week. Make sure to set up some time for rest, holidays, summer, and the like. But the aspects of this book that you put into practice are not short term. They take time to learn and make a part of everyday life. You don't have to reread the book over and over, but structure time around the aspects of worship, study, the three questions, storytelling, and prayer. Each of these aspects will be laid out and discussed in the pages that follow, and they'll help you set up a process for discipleship that fits your community and needs.

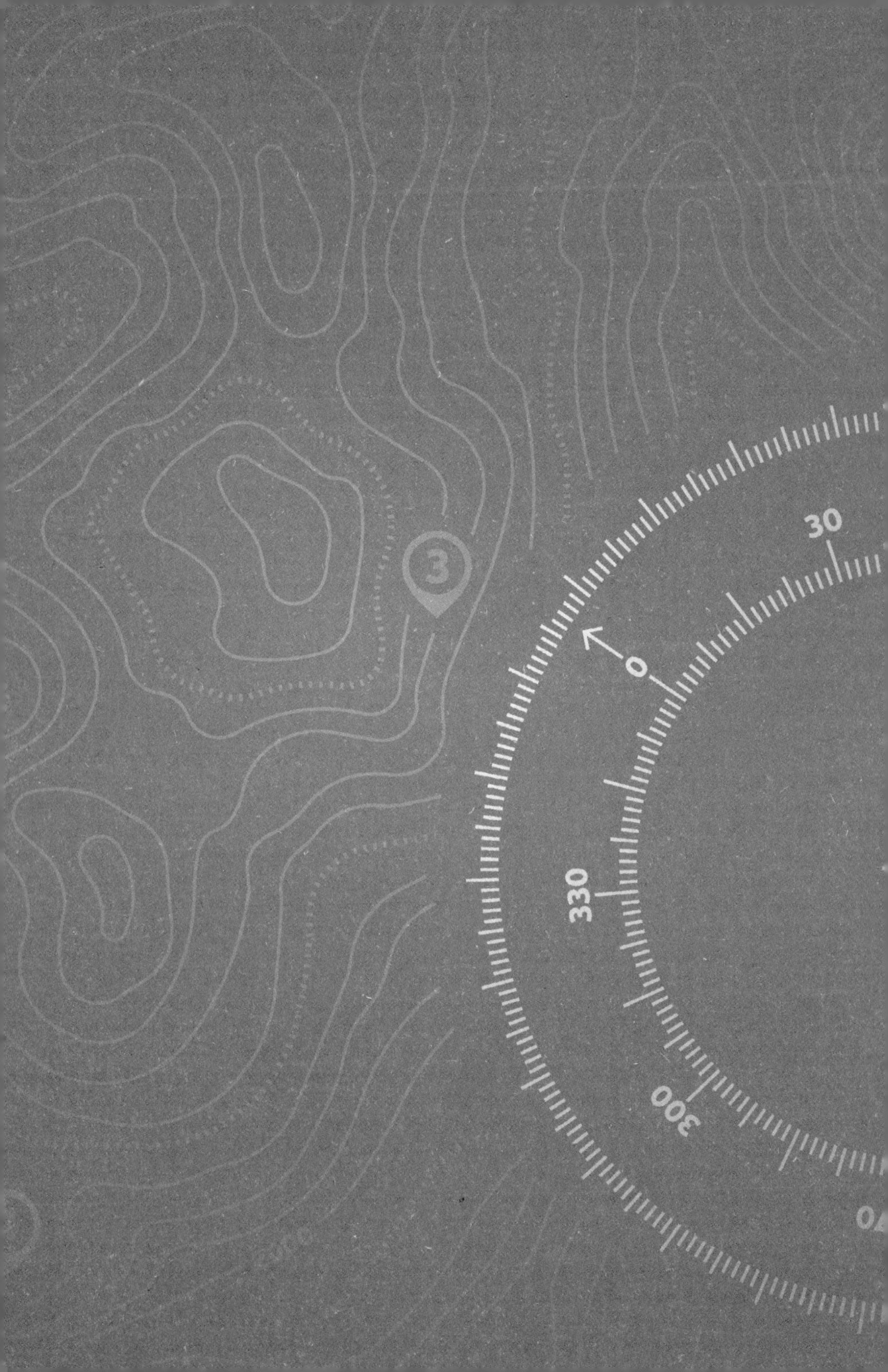
3
30
0
330
300

What Is a Disciple?

In the summer of 2016, my wife and I bought our first house. That summer, there was an incredibly high seller's market in our area. We had put in six offers on houses over a period of several months, only to have all of them rejected. Finally, our seventh offer was accepted. There is a picture of two young kids (us) standing in front of our new house with smiles wide enough to cross the Grand Canyon. It was another step toward adulthood; we were homeowners.

But do you know what comes with owning your own home? All. The. Maintenance. We were excited that our home was only two years old, a new build, and that it should be a good while before we had to do boring things like replace the condenser on the main unit of our AC system, or have the main circuit board of our AC system replaced, or pull out electrical sockets that had overloaded, or rent a giant dehumidifier from the hardware store because the washer had overflowed into the kitchen. (That last one was on me. Always, *always* replace the drainage pipe right away after you move the washer.)

My wife and I do love our house, but it has taken us time to get past some of the issues we didn't realize we would have. In the midst of all of these things happening, YouTube was an incredible resource. Most major housing issues and improvements have helpful guides posted on YouTube. When our first electrical outlet sputtered, fizzed, and then died, I was able to find a video online on how to replace it. That first fix was rough. There was yelling, clipping of wires too long, and realizing I had bought an outlet that was harder to install than I had planned—but finally, victory! The outlet was replaced!

Replacing the outlet gave me a great feeling of accomplishment . . . until the next outlet went out. Then it was back to the hardware store, though this time I did buy the right kind of replacement, and I cut both the yelling and installation time nearly in half. As I plugged in a lamp, the light radiated across my personal little victory!

Then, several weeks later, another outlet went out. This time I bought a ten-pack of replacements at the hardware store. I cut my repair time down again. But when I finished and felt accomplished, there was another idea in the back of my mind: my house might have received a bad batch of plugs, which meant more outlets were going to fail. When the next plug went out, however, I was able to replace it in five minutes with no yelling.

Fast-forward a couple of years, and I am still learning about home maintenance and updates. Through our neighborhood Facebook group, we were able to obtain around five hundred feet of free crown molding. After sanding, painting, and prepping, the molding was finally ready to go up. My dad and his friend Steve drove up from Houston to help us install the crown molding throughout the downstairs.

Within minutes of hanging the molding, we ran into our first problem: the ceiling in our dining room bowed downward along one wall. The molding didn't have enough bend to make it up into the corner. Then I watched as Steve and my dad worked some magic. By moving the conjoining molding an eighth of an inch here, a sixteenth of an inch there, they problem-solved that corner. I was dumbstruck with amazement. Here were two men who had been working on home improvement projects together for over fifteen years, and when they hit a snag, they just took it in stride.

Throughout the rest of the day, Steve walked me through the cuts he was making, how he was measuring, and tricks for how he planned out each step. Dad jumped into putting the finishing touches (caulking, filling holes, and a final coat of paint) on the molding. Along the way, he taught my brother (who had come over after work) and my wife to do what he was doing. Hanging and putting final touches on this molding took less than a day. The main reason it was done so quickly was that Steve and Dad walked alongside us and taught us as we went.

Before you go double-checking to make sure you picked up a book on discipleship and not home improvement, let me reassure you, this is all pertinent to our topic. Discipleship is a subject in the Church that covers a vast spectrum of ideas, practices, and principles. In an effort to continue in the commission Jesus gave us, we have built complex strategies for how best to "make disciples of all nations." Our faith journeys become lists of what we need to do to be "just a little better." We look ahead and think, "If only I can do _____, then I'll have made it." The problem is, once we make it there, we realize we haven't made it at all.

Discipleship should be simpler. Discipleship *is* simpler. It's like replacing an outlet or hanging crown molding.

First, there will always be problems. Jesus promised us in John 16:33, "In the world you will have tribulation." Discipleship is not accomplished on the first try. Often, it will take frustration, struggle, and possibly a bit of yelling. But the more you experience it, the more you learn and grow.

Second, Jesus has not left you without instruction. Scripture teaches and guides us. It gives us a light to follow in the darkness.

Finally, Jesus has not left you alone. There are people who have gone before you. They've dealt with the issues you are having. Their journey in faith benefits you. Paul calls on the Church at Corinth to imitate him as he imitates Christ. A good gift of God to the Church are those who have walked farther in faith. The journey of discipleship is about both being a disciple and seeking to disciple others.

The Basics

It is important for our discussion of discipleship to start with the basics. Discipleship is not some new concept that was pulled out of thin air. It is a core tenet of the Christian faith instituted by Jesus before He ascended to heaven. His followers have always gone out to make disciples. The twelve disciples we hear so much about in the New Testament took disciple making so seriously that many lost their lives because of it. Disciple making became part of their daily lives. They learned this from Jesus as He taught them while journeying around the countryside. Discipleship is an ancient piece of our faith that is lived out as we journey through life.

Nothing New

> And Jesus came and said to them, "All authority in heaven and on earth has been given to Me. Go therefore and make disciples of all nations, baptizing them in the name of the Father and of the Son and of the Holy Spirit, teaching them to observe all that I have commanded you. And behold, I am with you always, to the end of the age." (Matthew 28:18–20)

As Jesus ascends, He gives His followers this command: Go and make disciples. It is the last thing He tells those who have walked alongside Him through the years of His ministry, His death, and His resurrection. It is important. Breaking down each piece of this commission will give us some insight as we begin our dive into discipleship and disciple making.

Disciple making is not founded on works. Jesus starts by telling those following Him that all authority in heaven and on earth has been given to Him. He sets the stage. It is not about our will or our striving; it is all based upon the authority of Jesus.

In that authority, Jesus gives a command to those who would follow Him: Go and make disciples. This is not something that happens by accident. While the power comes from Jesus, He invites us to be an integral part of the process. The life of a Christian does not mean we sit on the sideline. We are called to be a part of the plan Jesus has to make more disciples!

Baptism is the beginning. What a wonderful gift! As humans, we constantly seek to measure up: Am I good enough? Do I have what it takes? What if people knew who I truly am? Jesus tells His followers to baptize more disciples. Why? Baptism is a gift of salvation where Jesus claims us as His own. Baptism brings us into the family of God. In that belonging, we are able to grow and explore what it means to be a family member. The lie that says we must first achieve some form of standing with God before we could possibly explore what it means to be part of the family is just that—a lie. You belong. There are no other requirements to live and grow as a disciple.

A life of discipleship is not easy. It will be full of mistakes and missteps. But Jesus gives us Baptism so that we do not despair. We are His children, bought at a price. The first mark of a disciple comes from outside the self. It is a sacramental gift Jesus gives to us. He claims us.

It is important for us to teach the ways and commands of God, but it is just as important to observe, or keep, those commands as fruit of the Spirit in our lives. Discipleship is not meant to be a life solely of study and reflection; it is meant to be lived out in daily life. Teaching gives us the basis for a life of discipleship, and observing and keeping those teachings walks them out into the world around us.

Making disciples is a daunting task, but Jesus gives us a peace-filled reminder: "I will be with you always." Discipleship and disciple making never happen alone. It is not based on us digging deep within ourselves. Instead, it is about remembering over and over again that our Savior walks with us as we go about a full life following Him. We are not alone.

The Disciples vs. a Disciple

There is a difference between *the* disciples and *a* disciple. As we dig deeper into ideas and concepts for disciple making and the life of discipleship, we are not trying to break into the category held by the twelve disciples who walked with Jesus during His time on earth.

Why even mention this distinction? The twelve disciples hold a mythic ideal in our heads. Truly, they were no different from you and me, save for the fact that they were chosen to be the ones who walked and lived in the closest proximity to Jesus during His ministry. But all Christians are called to be disciples. There are no prequalifying conditions for you to be a disciple aside from being a baptized member of the family of God.

The disciples went into the world to make many disciples. After Jesus' ascension, these men and those who followed along with them took the Great Commission seriously. They began making disciples throughout Jerusalem, Judea, Samaria, and to the ends of the earth. They knew how important disciple making is, and many of them gave their lives for the sake of the Kingdom because of it.

You will never be one of *the* disciples. Not because you aren't good enough, but because it is a definition that helps us identify a group of twelve. But you are *a* disciple in the same vein that they were. You are bought at a price. You have been called to be a messenger of the kingdom of God wherever you go.

Are We There Yet?

Are we there yet? That classic question often falls on parents as a refrain from their kids in the back seat. We, as adults, still ask it though; we just often internalize the question. Always we are looking to the finish line, looking for when we have "made it." This also happens in a life of discipleship. Often, Christians can find themselves asking, "Well, once I've got _____ under my belt, then I will have made it! I will be a disciple!"

Is this how discipleship shapes us in real life though? Do we work to follow Jesus, then hit the finish line and coast until He calls us home? It is a basic human instinct to want this to be true. *If I can only make it this far. . . . If I can only make it a few more steps. . . . Just focus on what's ahead, then maybe I can finally take a break.* Unfortunately, this leads to stagnation of faith. Instead of actually reaching that finish line on the other side, you will find there's just one thing more to do. Then just one more mile to go. Just one more goal to try to achieve.

What if, instead of viewing discipleship as a sprint, we viewed it as backpacking? Why do people take months to hike the Appalachian or Pacific Crest Trail? Don't these people know that you can drive to many of these places without the need to walk thousands of miles? When you are hiking, you notice the small things along the trail. That which hurts and is a struggle on day 1 becomes a distant memory, an experience the hiker draws wisdom from when facing new, tougher obstacles. Each day is filled with small steps toward a bigger goal. Mountaintops lead to valleys, which lead back to mountaintops, and on and on it goes with one foot in front of the other. Rather than "Are we there yet?" a disciple asks, "What will we experience as we go?"

Journey of Discipleship

Discipleship is the trail through the woods—the one where the traveler has to keep checking the map to keep from getting lost, only to get lost anyway. The path will continue through streams, muck, and rain, but it will also lead to grand mountain views, pleasant valleys, and still waters. Who and what, then, makes up this journey?

WHO

The people walking this journey are on it together. Throughout Scripture, we find the process of discipleship to be personal. It is first reflected in the Trinity.

The Father speaks of His love for the Son:

> And when Jesus was baptized, immediately He went up from the water, and behold, the heavens were opened to Him, and He saw the Spirit of God descending like a dove and coming to rest on Him; and behold, a voice from heaven said, "This is My beloved Son, with whom I am well pleased." (Matthew 3:16–17)

Jesus speaks about abiding in that love from the Father and how it glorifies God:

> If you abide in Me, and My words abide in you, ask whatever you wish, and it will be done for you. By this My Father is glorified, that you bear much fruit and so prove to be My disciples. As the Father has loved Me, so have I loved you. Abide in My love. If you keep My commandments, you will abide in My love, just as I have kept My Father's commandments and abide in His love. These things I have

spoken to you, that My joy may be in you, and that your joy may be full. (John 15:7–11)

The prophet Isaiah prophesied about the relationship Jesus would have with the Holy Spirit during His time on earth:

There shall come forth a shoot from the stump of Jesse, and a branch from his roots shall bear fruit. And the Spirit of the LORD shall rest upon Him, the Spirit of wisdom and understanding, the Spirit of counsel and might, the Spirit of knowledge and the fear of the LORD. And His delight shall be in the fear of the LORD. He shall not judge by what His eyes see, or decide disputes by what His ears hear, but with righteousness He shall judge the poor, and decide with equity for the meek of the earth; and He shall strike the earth with the rod of His mouth, and with the breath of His lips He shall kill the wicked. Righteousness shall be the belt of His waist, and faithfulness the belt of His loins. (Isaiah 11:1–5)

Discipleship is a journey started with the Godhead and built into the world around us. The Father as Creator put this into place as part of the redeeming plan that He would sacrifice His Son to enact. That salvation gives the believer access to the blessings of the Holy Spirit, who works to guide the followers of Jesus in loving God and loving their neighbors. The first "who" of discipleship is always God: what He has done and is doing in the lives of His people and the world.

Second, there is a blessing of another "who" on this journey. The Book of Hebrews explains them to us this way:

> Therefore, since we are surrounded by so great a cloud of witnesses, let us also lay aside every weight, and sin which clings so closely, and let us run with endurance the race that is set before us, looking to Jesus, the founder and perfecter of our faith, who for the joy that was set before Him endured the cross, despising the shame, and is seated at the right hand of the throne of God. (12:1–2)

The cloud of witnesses is set around us to be travel guides along this journey, to help one another endure for the long haul. In poetry, David declares, "One generation shall commend Your works to another, and shall declare Your mighty acts" (Psalm 145:4). It is part of the calling of the Body of Christ, the Church, to disciple in the ways of Jesus.

This is a gift of God. Those older or more seasoned in the journey of discipleship are called to be guides and mentors to those on the journey with them who have less experience. It is a form of apprenticeship. Those who have gone ahead on the trail don't stop and simply admire the view; they go back to help those who are journeying as well. They give them the tips and tricks, show them the way to read the map, encourage them through the tough switchbacks, and critique them along the way to help them stay on the trail. Discipleship is built to exist in community. It is a discipline meant to be shared. In our lives as followers of Jesus, we should always be looking for someone who can disciple us and for someone whom we might disciple.

HEAD

> The fear of the Lord is the beginning of wisdom,
> and the knowledge of the Holy One is insight.
> (Proverbs 9:10)

If discipleship is a journey, how do we know where to go? Building a knowledge base of who Jesus is, His promises, the ways of God, and how we interact with the world is an essential practice. The draw of the enemy will turn us inward and away from looking to Jesus. Growth as a disciple does contain aspects of personal, professional, and relational growth. God designed this journey for us to discover who we are created to be. However, when we make self-help our goal, we lose sight of where we are being called. Knowing the path keeps us from wandering away from Jesus and toward destruction.

Investing time in study of Scripture, doctrine, and theology is a major part of discipleship. Knowledge of God and who He is informs our journey. It's the map that keeps us on the trail, the guide that lets us know which berries are safe to eat and which need to be tossed away. It lets us know when we need to slow down or speed up.

Knowledge keeps us on the trail. It steers our journey to seek after God and not ourselves. It allows us to explore but not to lose our way in the darkness.

Founded in Scripture and the writings of the saints, knowledge of God must be a part of discipleship.

HEART

> With my whole heart I seek You; let me not wander
> from Your commandments! (Psalm 119:10)

The study of God alone is not enough; it must also become a part of our identity. The heart's interaction with the knowledge of God changes us. Transformation is part of the journey.

The grace made possible by the cross must transform our lives. The Gospel message that Jesus died at just the right time, while we were still sinners, cannot simply live on pages and in manuscripts. It is not just a knowledge we have but the truth we experience. If knowledge of God is our map, then experience of salvation is the purpose of the journey. Having a map is great, but if there is no reason to use it, then it's just another piece of paper. Knowledge of God seeps into our hearts by the gift of the Holy Spirit, giving purpose to the journey. As we grow in faith, the Holy Spirit works through knowledge to transform us and change who we are.

HANDS

But be doers of the word, and not hearers only, deceiving yourselves. (James 1:22)

Faith is not meant to exist only within ourselves. The knowledge of God moves into our identity and then out into the world as we interact with creation and our neighbors. The discipleship journey cannot exist only internally. If we are going to follow Jesus, we must put to rest the persistent heresy that the spiritual is somehow more holy than the physical. God is creator of both body and soul; He looks upon it all and says it is good. Therefore, discipleship cannot be allowed to remain only within ourselves; it is meant to be lived out wherever we go.

Our actions are an important part of our discipleship. Now, this does not mean that what we do saves us. God begins His work in us in our salvation, but He continues it until the day we die, with perfection arriving only at the second coming of Christ. Thus, what we do with our hands in the world around us matters for our life of discipleship.

Discipleship is about transformation, growing us into more committed followers of Jesus. This is played out in our actions in the world. Jesus has told us the two greatest commandments are to love God and to love our neighbors. That's it. Two simple ideas. On this journey, there must be progress. Sometimes it will be with heavy feet and labored breath, struggling to make it one more step. Other moments it will seem as if we are sprinting up the side of the mountain, overjoyed to see the work that God is doing in our lives. Worst of all, there will be times on this journey when we will pick ourselves up battered and bruised, having fallen down and rolled backward, losing ground instead of gaining it.

This is why discipleship must be an intermingling of head, heart, and hands. The Spirit takes our heads back time and again to the Word of God. As disciples, we are not to be normed by worldly forces. Instead, on our journey of discipleship, we constantly go back to the knowledge of God and who He is so that we may always be prepared to step outside of ourselves and not get caught in sinful ways, falsely believing that they are a form of following Jesus. The Spirit molds our hearts with that knowledge and transforms it into purpose and identity as the Word of God works in our lives. With our identity firmly rooted in faith and baptismal promise, knowledge of God doesn't grow stagnant but instead gives us fuel for following Jesus. Finally, the Spirit puts us to work in the world. Our hands are given to us so that we not only talk a good game but also live a life in the world that shows Jesus is leading us, so that others "may see your good works and give glory to your Father who is in heaven" (Matthew 5:16).

Head. Heart. Hands. All pieces of the whole discipleship journey.

Our Definition

What, then, is a disciple? A disciple is a person who trusts the promises of Jesus and seeks to follow Him. Simple.

(Trusting Jesus is where we start our discipleship journey.) Trying to walk this journey of our own will and strength means failure is ahead. However, the promises of Jesus deeply root the foundation and identity of a disciple in the Gospel. A disciple can be constantly renewed and challenged to keep that trust strong through worshiping with the Body of Christ, through the Word, and in the Sacraments.

Seeking Jesus must also be a part of the discipleship journey. Those who stop seeking will stagnate and stop moving along the path. Community is an incredible gift that helps keep us moving forward. Hearing the voice of God through His Word and a few simple steps will benefit disciples as they move forward on the journey.

Following Jesus where He is leading can be one of the hardest parts of discipleship. This will mean taking the promises of Jesus that form our identity, connecting them to a life of seeking His will through His Word, and walking it into the world around us. Your story, empowered by prayer, will help you to tell Jesus' story through both your words and actions. The vocation of every disciple is to follow Jesus wherever He is leading.

This book will be a mix of head, heart, and hands. Throughout, you will find writings to challenge you in those areas, along with disciplines you can use to grow in your discipleship journey. Again, I encourage you: do not read this book alone. Instead, bring together a group of family or friends. Walk the journey together.

Read this book with an open Bible. This book isn't meant to be revolutionary, but it will bring you back to an idea: the journey of discipleship is simple, yet it may be the hardest thing you do in your life. It is day in and day out. Extraordinary and mundane. Mountaintops, valleys, and everything in between. The Word of God will be your help and guide through it all. Long after the name of this book is forgotten to history, God's Word will remain steadfast. Keep it at hand. Maybe this process is nothing new, but you are looking for a fresh set of eyes to see the trail. Great! This book is not the be-all and end-all of discipleship. In fact, it is just a set of tools to help you along the way.

A journey begins with one step. There will be temptation to make this book a destination. "Once I've read this book on discipleship, then I will have made it." Try not to do that. Instead, take a deep breath and look at the trail ahead. There will be beauty, there will be rocky ground, there will be blood, sweat, and tears. But don't focus on the end. Start with one step. Then another. Next thing you know, you will have found your stride. Be challenged, look deep, and keep moving forward.

DISCIPLESHIP COMMUNITY

OPEN WITH PRAYER

Ask for a volunteer to open with prayer. Rotate who does this each time you get together. Praying in front of people may scare you, but it is worth growing in the practice. Praying together is part of what the Body of Christ does. Not only is it our connection to God but it also gives an example of how we live on this discipleship journey.

INTRODUCTIONS

Get to know one another! Discipleship includes walking together shoulder to shoulder as you go. Here are a few example questions.

- If you could go anywhere for a week, all expenses paid, where would you go? Why?

- What is one thing you've never done but always wanted to do?

- Dogs or cats?

DISCUSSION

1. As you read the definition of a disciple, what stood out to you?

2. What do you think of when you hear the word *disciple*? Do you consider yourself a disciple?

3. What do you think of the idea of discipleship?

4. This chapter talked about the definitions of *discipleship* and *disciple* and also presented the basic understanding of discipleship as a journey rather than a destination. What are your thoughts on these things?

5. What challenges do you expect when starting this journey?

6. What do you want to get out of this journey?

CLOSING

Set a time for when you will get together again. Getting on a regular schedule is an investment that will pay off in the long run.

Pray for one another. Take prayer requests and close in prayer. Spread out the prayer requests so as many people are praying as are available.

BEFORE NEXT TIME

Read the "Trust" devotion and chapter 2 and prepare answers for the questions.

Trust

The Lord is not slow to fulfill His promise as some count slowness, but is patient toward you, not wishing that any should perish, but that all should reach repentance.

2 Peter 3:9

Now that we have defined a disciple as a person who trusts the promises of Jesus and seeks to follow Him, let's spend time breaking that down. The sections of this book focus on trusting, seeking, and following Jesus. Before each section, there will be a short devotional moment like this one to help you slow down and reflect on the idea. Then, each chapter will address different aspects of that part of the discipleship journey. Every chapter interacts with the others and is part of the whole.

Trusting the promises of Jesus is a paradoxical concept. In the coming chapters, you will read about *you* trusting. Yet, trusting the promises of Jesus will always come back to the greatest promise: the Gospel—that Jesus would die for us. Trust in this promise is a gift of the Holy Spirit bound in the Word that gives us faith. Is it truly, then, our trust that binds us to these promises—or are the promises binding our trust to them?

Yes.

That is the paradox. Two seemingly contradictory ideas that at the same time are both true. We trust God, but at the same time that trust is created by God. If you can't wrap your mind around it, that is okay. The point is that trusting Jesus is the key component in the discipleship journey. Trust is a beautiful paradox that blesses the Christian with assurance in what Jesus says.

As you read the rest of this book, trust will always be in the background. It is the main thing. Jesus is for us; His promises are what grant us salvation and new life. Because this trust is a cornerstone, it will also play a role in seeking and following. Never throw this idea away. God is working in and empowering us through Jesus' promises in which we trust.

Paradox is not bad. It is just something that we struggle to explain. But there is beauty in it. If we knew all the ways in which God worked, what kind of God would He be? Paradox allows us to see that as God works, there will be both knowns and unknowns.

Before you begin these chapters, take a moment to jot down some promises of Jesus that you know. Write out the significance of them. Why are they important? Take a look at those promises from both a wider perspective and a personal view: Why is this promise important to all people? What does it mean for me?

If you are reading this book in a group, share together those promises you wrote down. Discuss how they play out in the world and in your life.

Lord, let me not forget the love You have for me. Even as I am on the journey of discipleship, remind me that my works are not what saves me. Show me Your grace and mercy. Bring me back to put my trust in You. Amen.

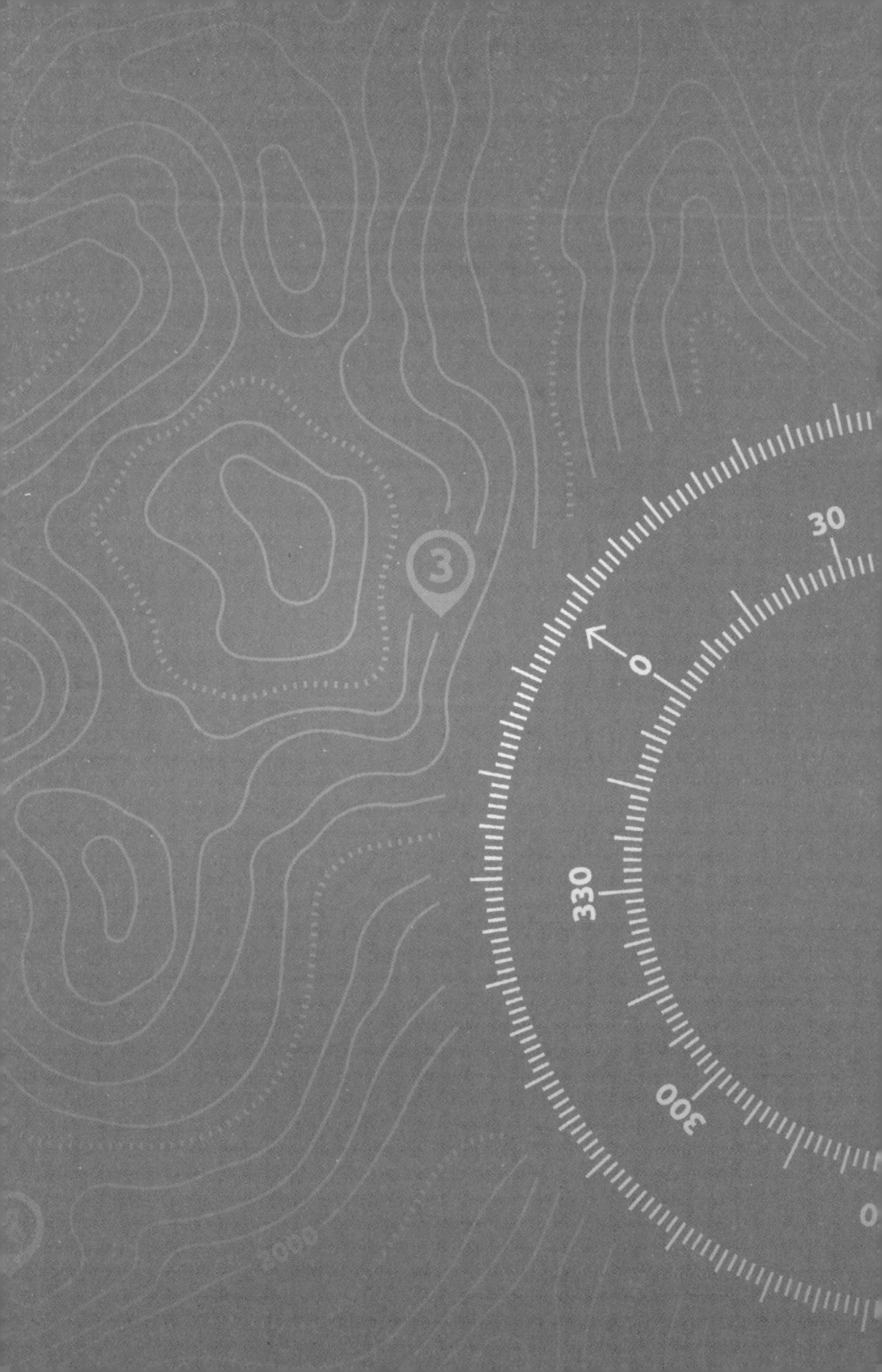
3
30
0
330
300

The Promises of Jesus

What is your dream car? Most people of driving age, many even before that time of their lives, have picked out the car that they feel fits them best. For some, it may be a classic restored muscle car from a time when Detroit was putting race cars in the hands of Americans. Others seek the comfort of leather seats and a smooth ride. Some dream of the truck or Jeep in which they can ford a river or travel rocky paths. Today, you may dream of a car that plugs in and autopilot you to your destination. Now imagine you are given that car, free of charge! You drive it around, excited to check out every bell and whistle. Then you find the longest, straightest stretch of road to really take it up to speed. You roll down the windows and the wind whistles as a smile stretches across your face.

But one thing is true about a car. It needs fuel. You pull up, proud of your new vehicle, and without paying attention, you fill it to the brim before heading back out. As you are getting down the road, your car starts to sputter. Your brand-new dream car! Suddenly, with a loud noise, it seems to lock up and you are just barely able to pull off the highway and call for a tow truck. Your mechanic gets back to you as quickly as possible. While you were beaming at the gas station, proud of your new car, you must have grabbed the diesel nozzle by mistake. Your brand-new dream machine is now due for some maintenance.

Now imagine that instead of mistakenly choosing diesel, you intentionally said, "Well, I know better than the manufacturer, and this car actually needs diesel." Or better yet, you found some way to shove a gas nozzle into your electric car to try to fill it up. Your dream car has just become a fancy rolling hunk of metal.

Discipleship is an amazing gift of God designed to be fueled in a specific way. The power of being a disciple of Jesus comes from one place: Jesus. Yet, stubbornness and self-idolization create a form of power that tries to replace that source. The first steps in discipleship must be to recognize that the energy needed to walk this journey comes from outside of us, not inside. It is not about finding the strength within ourselves but rather about receiving the gift God has given that fuels our journey—the gift of the Gospel.

The Gospel

The journey of discipleship is given its lasting power from the work of Jesus. Jesus' purpose in coming down from heaven was to redeem creation back to God. The Good News, the Gospel, is that Jesus came while humanity was still broken, while it was still sinful, while it could do nothing, and He did everything. He took the sins of the world upon Himself and carried that burden up a hill in Israel to be executed because He threatened the religious leaders and was a rabble-rouser to the imperial authorities. But it gets even better. Jesus' teachings were, and still are, revolutionary. His wisdom sought to seek and serve those He deemed "the least of these." He made the rich and wise feel poor and foolish. He made the brokenhearted whole. On the cross, He did more. He took the sin we could not pay for and let it land on His shoulders. He took our evil and let it become His. He saw the darkness of our hearts and still He cried, "It is finished."

No matter what you have done, no matter what you will do, you cannot run away from the love that was purchased for you on a hill in the Middle East all those years ago. The Good News doesn't stop there. Jesus' story doesn't stop there. Three days later, women came to His tomb, seeking to anoint His body. They found that the cave where He had been laid was empty. Jesus' death declares the forgiveness of sins. His resurrection gives us new life. The Gospel is both of those things: freedom from sin and the joy of a new life.

The power of discipleship comes from this work of Jesus for us. It is not personal power or good works that fuel this journey. No, it is the work of Jesus. That is why trusting the promises of Jesus is the first step down this pathway.

The Promises of Jesus

(The definition of a disciple is a person who trusts the promises of Jesus and seeks to follow Him.)Trusting the promises of Jesus is the fuel for this journey. It is the core identity of a disciple. The beauty of these promises is that they start at salvation!

JUSTIFICATION

For God so loved the world, that He gave His only Son, that whoever believes in Him should not perish but have eternal life. For God did not send His

Son into the world to condemn the world, but in
order that the world might be saved through Him.
(John 3:16–17)

Jesus' greatest promise is that His death justifies humanity
before God. This brings us back to the Gospel, that great fuel
of the faith. This fuel for the disciple is like jet fuel. It must be
the core of everything that happens on the discipleship journey.
Drinking deep from the living waters of this promise empowers
the disciple. It cannot be overemphasized that this is where the
beginning and end of the Christian faith is found. Over and
over again, a disciple must return to this promise.

When a disciple turns away, justification is there. Paul wrote
to the Church in Rome to tell them that "while we were still
weak, at the right time Christ died for the ungodly" (Romans
5:6). There will be innumerable times in the journey of discipleship when the path is left behind, idols are chased, or self-righteousness becomes the norm. The wayward disciple finds redemption at its source—the promise of justification. To return
is to trust the promise for you. The gift of the only Son brings
forgiveness as a balm to the sickness of the sinful human con-
dition. It not only heals but also strengthens. This promise tears
down idols and selfishness, revealing a Savior who not only
takes our mistakes but also receives our willful disobedience.

Justification brings comfort to the downtrodden. Life on
the path of discipleship will bring hardships and heartaches,
many of which come about simply because this world is full of
sin. Death, difficulty, and tragedy may be around any bend as
the disciple travels through this world. But this promise is made
perfect in weakness; its grace is sufficient. Justification brings

hope to the hopeless and help to the helpless. It is a beacon in the dark night of the soul by which Jesus declares that all is not lost. Salvation is not only about the kingdom of God to which we will one day be resurrected but also about that Kingdom breaking into our world. Jesus tells us that the kingdom of God is at hand, that it has come near. That Kingdom comes to us through Jesus, through His work on the cross and His defeat of death in the empty tomb. Our hope is anchored there; that is where the broken find comfort.

Abiding and Bearing Fruit

Abide in Me, and I in you. As the branch cannot bear fruit by itself, unless it abides in the vine, neither can you, unless you abide in Me. I am the vine; you are the branches. Whoever abides in Me and I in him, he it is that bears much fruit, for apart from Me you can do nothing. If anyone does not abide in Me he is thrown away like a branch and withers; and the branches are gathered, thrown into the fire, and burned. If you abide in Me, and My words abide in you, ask whatever you wish, and it will be done for you. By this My Father is glorified, that you bear much fruit and so prove to be My disciples. (John 15:4–8)

Come to Me, all who labor and are heavy laden, and I will give you rest. Take My yoke upon you, and learn from Me, for I am gentle and lowly in heart, and you will find rest for your souls. For My yoke is easy, and My burden is light. (Matthew 11:28–30)

Justification is the beginning promise, but God continues to give us good gifts. Throughout Scripture, Jesus often speaks of abiding and bearing fruit. Again, disciples can fall into the trap of believing it is their work that strengthens them for the journey. Abiding and bearing fruit is the promise that brings us back to the heart of what Jesus is doing. Look at the above verses from John 15. The promise of abiding is that those who do will bear fruit. The promise of justification is passive; you don't do anything! As Jesus keeps His promises in justification, He invites you to join in His work by abiding in Him, which contains a secondary promise: that you will bear fruit.

Think about how fruit grows. Fruit bushes and trees don't make a conscious decision to grow fruit; it's just part of what they do. Jesus' promise is that if we abide in Him, we will grow fruit. Now, if you were to go back to John 15:1, you would find that Jesus says He is the vine and His Father is the vinedresser—someone who cultivates and cares for the plants. This promise lets us know that abiding will bring with it pruning; if there are branches in the life of a disciple that are not producing fruit, they will be pruned—and not only pruned but burned in fire (John 15:6). The proof of a disciple is in the fruit he or she bears.

Too often, disciples look to their fruit as evidence of their faith. When the temptation comes to look at the fruit, we must remember that every promise Jesus gives cannot and will not contradict another. Fruit is indeed a marker of abiding, and part of the process of bearing good fruit is pruning. A lack of fruit, or perhaps some sour fruit, does not automatically mean our justification is in question. Rather, it is a warning sign to us. Bearing fruit isn't simply about producing; it is an indicator of health. When a disciple begins to see a lack of fruit, it is not a time to question, "Am I possibly saved?" Instead, it is time to return to the vine, to rest and abide in the foundational promise of Jesus' work of justification. Temptation will lead disciples to try to dig deeper in themselves, to try to prove their worth. However, what if instead we understood these as warning signs, symptoms that point to a deeper sickness, rot that can be solved only by the vinedresser?

Reality and Hope

> I have said these things to you, that in Me you may have peace. In the world you will have tribulation. But take heart; I have overcome the world. (John 16:33)

This world will bring trouble. That is one of the more intense promises of Jesus. He does not pull any punches. Paul called it "this present darkness" (Ephesians 6:12). It is important for disciples to recognize that Jesus makes this declaration. The life of following after Him will not be without trial and tribulation. In fact, while His yoke and burden are easy because of our redemption through His work on the cross, this life of following after Him will be the hardest thing His followers do. Too often, disciples are fooled by the lie that walking the journey will be easy, flat, and full of wonder. But what about the times when doubt arises? when sickness takes the ones we love? when the money seems to be running out? when tragedy strikes? when it's just a regular Monday?

Discipleship is not about wearing rose-colored glasses. Instead, discipleship means seeing the reality of this world but placing our hope in Jesus. Immediately after the promise of hardship in this world, Jesus makes a more powerful promise: "But take heart; I have overcome the world." If disciples were to end the journey anytime they encountered hardship, there would be no one who walked this path. But in this promise of Jesus, reality is tempered with hope. There will be hardship, but He has overcome it all.

The Helper

> These things I have spoken to you while I am still with you. But the Helper, the Holy Spirit, whom the Father will send in My name, He will teach you all things and bring to your remembrance all that I have said to you. Peace I leave with you; My peace I give to you. Not as the world gives do I give to you. Let not your hearts be troubled, neither let them be afraid. (John 14:25–27)

> And when they bring you before the synagogues and the rulers and the authorities, do not be anxious about how you should defend yourself or what you should say, for the Holy Spirit will teach you in that very hour what you ought to say. (Luke 12:11–12)

Jesus does not leave you alone. The promise of the Holy Spirit is a gift to all who are baptized and trust in His name. Often referred to as the Helper, the Spirit will move in our lives on a daily basis. This promise of Jesus brings with it conviction and growth. The Helper teaches, reminds, and brings us peace.

The Holy Spirit teaches the ways of Jesus through encouragement and conviction. In line upon line and verse after verse, the Holy Spirit works through Scripture to communicate with the people of God. Encouragement is mixed with conviction, and the steadfast love of God is mixed with the call to return to the rhythms of life in which God designed humanity to live. Learning to hear the Holy Spirit through God's Word will be a lifelong pursuit of a disciple. It will bring encouragement to the downtrodden, conviction to the comfortable, and the clear message to all of the need for a Savior and a call to live as God created us to live. Hold on to this idea—it will be discussed in more depth in a later chapter.

"The Holy Spirit . . . [will] bring to your remembrance all that I have said to you." These words are the deep well of grace breaking through the ground to form the spring of life in the journey of discipleship. Trust in the promises of Jesus is found in this one sentence. The Holy Spirit will daily bring the remembrance of the gift of salvation found in Jesus, that deepest of promises sealed in Baptism. Chief among the teachings of Jesus is salvation. Yet, the Helper will not stop there. A remembrance of all that Jesus has said will be brought to light again and again. From the whisperings of the Spirit, disciples will be brought back to the Beatitudes, the greatest commandments, the many teachings and promises of Jesus.

Peace that passes understanding radiates from the promised Helper. Jesus' encouragement to His first followers in Luke 12 is the promise of peace. These followers will be brought before important people, even though their stations in life do not warrant the audience, but they will have peace. The Holy

Spirit will speak for them. How often in this journey do disciples find themselves worried about saying or doing the right thing? Will their words muddle their confession of who Jesus is? The promised Helper will guide them and bring peace to these moments—and not only that, but peace in trials, peace in heartache. The Holy Spirit delivers the balm of the Gospel to the disciple in those times of conviction, which in turn leads to a peace that cannot be found outside of Jesus. The amazing promises of Jesus continually lead us back to Him! In the work of the Holy Spirit, this promised Helper, Jesus grants us the gift of peace. Peace in a world that is troubled. Peace for a world that has strayed from Him. Peace for the disciple who follows Him.

The Kingdom

Therefore I tell you, do not be anxious about your life, what you will eat or what you will drink, nor about your body, what you will put on. Is not life more than food, and the body more than clothing? Look at the birds of the air: they neither sow nor reap nor gather into barns, and yet your heavenly Father feeds them. Are you not of more value than they? And which of you by being anxious can add a single hour to his span of life? And why are you anxious about clothing? Consider the lilies of the field, how they grow: they neither toil nor spin, yet I tell you, even Solomon in all his glory was not arrayed like one of these. But if God so clothes the grass of the field, which today is alive and tomorrow is thrown into the oven, will He not much more clothe you, O you of little faith? Therefore do not be anxious, saying, "What shall we eat?" or "What shall we drink?" or "What shall we wear?" For the Gentiles seek after all these things, and your heavenly Father knows that you need them all. But seek first the kingdom of God and His righteousness, and all these things will be added to you. Therefore do not be anxious about tomorrow, for tomorrow will be anxious for itself. Sufficient for the day is its own trouble. (Matthew 6:25–34)

Jesus promises the kingdom of God. Let that sink it.

Jesus promises that the rule and reign of the Creator of the universe has come. When He started His earthly ministry, He declared, "The time is fulfilled, and the kingdom of God is at hand; repent and believe in the gospel" (Mark 1:15). Let's break that down: The time is fulfilled. Finally, the promised Messiah that the people of God have been waiting for is at work among them. He is beginning His work in the created world. Next, He declares that the kingdom of God is at hand. What is the kingdom of God? How can He declare it at hand? Well, the Kingdom is always first and foremost wherever the King is. When Jesus proclaims the Kingdom being at hand, He is speaking literally. For the first time since the Garden, when God walked with Adam and Eve, the created can reach out and touch the Creator. When Jesus tells them the kingdom of God is at hand, He means it! Reach out and touch the King and you will be touching the Kingdom. Repent and believe this good news. Turn from the old ways of the world. Reach out for the kingdom of God.

For disciples, this is an incredible promise. Reach out for the Kingdom and it will be found. In the above section of

Matthew 6, this promise works itself out for all those who follow Jesus. Look at the first section of that passage. Jesus understands the worries of this world. He knows that there will be fears and anxieties, but the promise comes with the Kingdom. "But seek first the kingdom of God and His righteousness, and all these things will be added to you" (v. 33). When the journey veers into the unknown and unexpected, disciples are given a promise for resolution: "Seek first the Kingdom." And what does that Kingdom look like? It is a Kingdom not of this world, a Kingdom where creation is made new, where there will be no more tears, and where everything will be as it was created to be. Right now, we see it through a mirror dimly. But when disciples encounter the anxious and fear-inducing current world and lift their eyes and set their faces toward the Kingdom, Jesus promises to provide.

What, then, does it mean to seek the Kingdom? How do disciples do this? They walk the discipleship journey, trusting, seeking, and following.

For some, the journey of life and discipleship carries with it debilitating anxiety and depression. Unfortunately, Matthew 6 has been used to pressure the anxious and depressed, as if those feelings could simply be fixed by having more faith. Some will say, "Just seek harder, trust deeper, and Jesus will take all of this from you." Except Jesus doesn't say to simply run from anxiety or depression; He calls the anxious and depressed to run to Him and His promise. Struggling with anxiety and depression does not mean you need to try harder in order to rid yourself of those feelings. Instead, rest in Him who promised that He has overcome the trouble you will have in this world. That is what it means to seek the Kingdom: Receive His promise, rest in His rule and reign, and lean into the grace poured over you in your Baptism. Dive deep into His gifts. Flee to them. Let the waters of the Gospel wash over you anew. The Kingdom can be sought because the King is at hand, reaching out to you.

To the End of the Age

> And Jesus came and said to them, "All authority in heaven and on earth has been given to Me. Go therefore and make disciples of all nations, baptizing them in the name of the Father and of the Son and of the Holy Spirit, teaching them to observe all that I have commanded you. And behold, I am with you always, to the end of the age." (Matthew 28:18–20)

By the time of this passage, Jesus has already promised the Holy Spirit, but He goes one step further. He promises that He will always walk with His disciples. He does not abandon disciples on their journey. He is not a worthless idol that must be visited at the high places. Instead, He is with His people. Wherever they go, whatever they do, He walks with them. Never alone, the disciple walks with the King.

Returning to the promises of Jesus fuels the disciple on the journey, beginning and ending with the promise of justification found in the death and resurrection of the Savior. When disciples find their trust in the promises of Jesus, there is power in the journey. This list of promises is also not the end. James reminds that "every good gift and every perfect gift is from above, coming down from the Father of lights, with whom there is no variation or shadow due to change" (1:17). This list is the starting point. Diving into the Gospels, we find more promises in the parables, the Sermon on the Mount, and the many times Jesus teaches to the crowd. But the promises must be that in which disciple place their trust. Not in their own works, for that fuel will fail them.

When the Promises Are Absent

If the works of a disciple are used as fuel for the journey, it will lead to exhaustion and wandering off the path. There is temptation to try to complicate discipleship by making it *solely* about the discipline of how discipleship is done. When the works of discipleship become the main fuel for discipleship, we lose sight of the deep power found in the Gospel. The complications of that line of thinking turn discipleship into hoops to be jumped through to try to reach some form of spiritual nirvana.

Exhaustion will be the new norm if discipleship is based on personal work. The enemy will tempt disciples toward doing all of this work of their own volition, whispering that lie, "If only you are a little bit better, then Jesus will love you more. If you would just do the things you are supposed to, then you would be a better Christian." There is only one thing that can make a person a better Christian, and that is the declaration that Jesus made on the cross. He sacrificed His life for you. When the enemy is able to pull our focus away from the promises of Jesus, he rips us away from the fuel and foundation of discipleship. It does not mean that those things have been taken from the followers of Jesus. The stream remains constantly present and ready to refresh the weary. But rather than take a drink, the temptation will be to say, "Once I have walked another two miles, I will have earned the drink. If I can only show one more fellow traveler the way, then I can drink deep. I will be worthy." Then, instead of finding refreshment, disciples will exhaust themselves. Discipleship cannot find its fuel and replenishment from working harder or doing better. Instead, disciples must return over and over again to the source.

Another danger when we don't return to Jesus' promises on the discipleship journey is wandering away from the path and into the wilderness of self. Unfortunately, there are many forms and methods of discipleship that push away from loving God and neighbor but forge instead toward a love of self. When the journey is founded on our own strength, we disciples slide down a slippery slope of seeking inward worthiness instead of seeking the Savior. This often manifests in a form of prosperity discipleship that focuses on the destiny of the disciple over all other things.

This is dangerous because it not only leads away from the greatest commandments but it often brings about hopelessness. If the source of discipleship is from within and not the promises of Jesus, then loving God and others becomes about what God and others can bring to the table. This focus disguises itself as bringing glory to God but ends up as seeking glorification for the disciple. With that focus, one seeks to be obedient to God because of what God will grant. It replaces love of neighbor with a self-centered love of what serving others will give to the servant.

When the disciple is lost in this wilderness of self-focus, hopelessness is right around the corner. If you are the center, you will fail. What happens when the trials come? What happens when the "promised" destiny does not happen? Hopelessness begins to slink its way into the soul. If there is one thing proven again and again in both Scripture and human nature, it is that people fail. People are not strong enough on their own to sustain hope in the face of those failures. Sadly, this hopelessness often leads to wandering not only from the path of discipleship but also away from faith entirely.

Daily Returning to the Promises

So how does a disciple trust in the promises of Jesus? Would that not in and of itself be a work? Yes and no. Does it take action to return to these promises? Yes. But is the disciple the one fulfilling those promises? No. These promises are given for this purpose: trusting in them is trusting in Jesus. The disciple returns to these promises—hourly, daily, weekly, monthly, yearly—a rhythm of coming back time and again to be refueled.

Trusting in self over these promises leads to disaster. The journey of discipleship will be fraught with despair and fatigue. But every disciple, because of human nature, will be pulled in this direction. This is why it is essential to keep returning to the promises of Jesus. The very nature of humanity will work against the disciple. When signs that we are wandering in the wilderness begin to appear, we will be tempted to languish in failure; the snare is set. Instead, return to the promise! Use those signs not for self-flagellation but to run back to the ever-flowing stream. Disciples do not need to walk the extra miles; the fuel is there. Stop and be energized by the promises of Jesus. Place trust outside of self and in the Savior.

The Power in the Promise

It is simple. The power for discipleship comes from the promises of Jesus. There is no other way around it. It cannot come from some other idea or striving. It starts at justification. Jesus is the King who entered the world to die for His people and rose again to show them the power He has to give them new life. These promises must be the central core of discipleship. There is no way they can be put anywhere else.

What is the purpose of the discipleship journey? We have defined *disciple*, but what about where this pathway leads? The short answer is to seek the Kingdom in everything. But what does that mean on Monday when the theory of discipleship becomes the reality of life? Each disciple must answer that in his or her own way. There is the path to follow—love God and love neighbors—but the beauty of these promises from Jesus is that they allow the answer to this question to be as unique as the person created to answer it. The potential is limitless when we trust these promises. The answer to this question is bound only by two other questions: Does it love God? Does it love my neighbor? If the answer to those is yes, then it is a purpose of the discipleship journey! We are not confined to a cookie-cutter idea of some super Christian; instead, discipleship powered by those promises allows us to pursue loving God and others wherever the opportunity arises!

Disciples will run into doubts. Good. Because the only way to overcome doubts is to realize that in weakness there is strength. Jesus provides the power. His promises run deep into the soul, fueling it in ways that were unimaginable.

For this reason I bow my knees before the Father, from whom every family in heaven and on earth is named, that according to the riches of His glory He may grant you to be strengthened with power through His Spirit in your inner being, so that Christ may dwell in your hearts through faith—that you, being rooted and grounded in love, may have strength to comprehend with all the saints what is the breadth and length and height and depth, and to know the love of Christ that surpasses knowledge, that you may be filled with all the fullness of God. Now to Him who is able to do far more abundantly than all that we ask or think, according to the power at work within us, to Him be glory in the church and in Christ Jesus throughout all generations, forever and ever. Amen. (Ephesians 3:14–21)

DISCIPLESHIP COMMUNITY

OPEN WITH PRAYER

Ask for a volunteer to open with prayer. Rotate who does this each time you get together. Praying in front of people may scare you, but it is worth growing in the practice. Praying together is part of what the Body of Christ does. Not only is it our connection to God but it also gives an example of how we live on this discipleship journey.

DISCUSSION

1. What jumped out to you in this chapter?

2. What is your dream car? Why?

3. Have you ever had a moment in your faith life when you leaned on yourself or your good works as justification for your salvation? How did that feel?

4. How does justification change your outlook on the discipleship journey?

5. Other than justification, which promise jumped out to you the most? Why?

DO IT

Learning to abide in Jesus is an important discipline as you grow. Take a minute with the group to discuss the differences between good fruit and bad fruit. What are you producing? What are examples of each in your life?

Throughout this week, whenever you notice bad fruit in your life, stop and abide. Read Psalm 23 and say a short prayer. Be ready to share next week how this happened throughout the week. Helpful hint: have someone in the group set up email reminders to help you pay attention to this during the week.

CLOSING

Make sure you know when you are getting together next.

Pray for one another. Take prayer requests and close in prayer. Spread out the prayer requests so as many people are praying as are available.

BEFORE NEXT TIME

Read chapter 3, prepare answers for the questions, and watch for your bad fruit in order to stop and abide!

Worship

GPS can be a funny thing. One November, my wife and I took a vacation to the Great Smoky Mountains National Park. We broke the trip into several legs, so we ended up entering the park on the Tennessee side after spending time with friends in Nashville. We plugged the campground location into our phones and followed the directions toward our destination. Great Smoky Mountains National Park is a little different from other parks we have experienced. While there are main gates, this park has many smaller back road accesses that are buried in the foothills. I started to get a little nervous as a turn that I imagined was taking us into the park itself suddenly popped up an hour and a half from our destination. Where was this taking us?

As we drove the back roads, a beautiful picture slowly began to appear before us. These country roads wound through foothills. Picturesque farms dotted the landscape. The cool November air had begun to transform the foliage to dark reds and vibrant golds. Driving farther, we passed out of the fields and into the forest. It was a surprise when we drove by what appeared to be an old metal street sign that read, "Now entering Great Smoky Mountains National Park." No large sign, not even a pull-off to get a picture next to. We were a little disappointed.

Then we crossed the bridge over the Little River. Along the Little River Gorge Road, the forest opened up from densely packed undergrowth to towering hardwoods whose overhanging branches created a cathedral over the winding road. Mountains shot up next to us and the clear waters of the Little River roared on the other side. The beauty and majesty of creation overwhelmed us. We found ourselves constantly catching our breath. As we set up our tent along the river that night, we were excited for the rest of our week.

And shouldn't that be how worship affects disciples? A planned route set up by the one who knows the way leads us back to the beauty of the promises of Jesus, which propel us into a life of discipleship. Worship is a gift from God to those who believe in Him, designed to bring the promises of Jesus to His people. It is built around delivering His promises while leaving room for us to respond. Call and response—God's promises, our joy in receiving them.

Worship is a routine that builds disciples as they navigate the world. Worship should have daily, weekly, and stretched-out components. It can be both gathered in the Body of Christ and scattered in the individual communities that make up a local church. There should be aspects that are deeply personal, hard to share with others. Yet it should also be incredibly communal, built around a group of people who are trusting, seeking, and following Jesus together. Worshiping happens across all of these avenues, and it is important for the disciple to engage in all of them.

The Worship Service

A close friend and elder at our church often reminded me on Sunday mornings of a simple fact: it's not called a worship service because we are here to serve God; He has called us together to serve us. How incredible is that one statement? In the long line of idols from the ancients until now, the local gods always demand sacrifice and adoration, as if they gain some sort of power by making people bow to them. The Creator of the universe, the true God, acts differently. He is filled with the awe, power, and authority that is always met with the phrase "Do not be afraid" when His followers meet Him. Yet, in His divine service to us, He steps down and meets us as we gather. Christians do not hold worship services to somehow fill God's battery that has been waning because it's been a week since people sang His praises. No; instead, He meets us in the service. He steps down and is among His people. Another promise of Jesus: "For where two or three are gathered in My name, there am I among them" (Matthew 18:20). God comes to serve His gathered people.

Coming together as God's people is important. In our culture, this is often on Sunday mornings, but sometimes it happens on an evening during the week. No matter when it happens, it is the people of God gathering together to receive His promises. Some people would say they do not need the gathering, that they can experience God on their own. While this does hold some truth—God may be experienced anywhere in His creation when connected to Scripture—it is not the way worship was designed to function. Since the beginning of the Christian Church, there has been gathering: "And they devoted themselves to the apostles' teaching and the fellowship, to the breaking of bread and the prayers" (Acts 2:42). It started in homes; when these gatherings outgrew homes and the government allowed them, Christians built houses of worship. Some of these great edifices can still be found dotting the landscapes of the Mediterranean today.

Gathering together as the Body of Christ in the name of Jesus has always been important. Community built around worship is the spiritual colliding with the physical. Songs are sung, prayers are prayed, sermons are preached, the Word is read, Sacraments are received. Alongside this beautiful mystery, coffee is shared, stories are told, friends catch up. Once a week, the Body of Christ is called together to be called back to their identity as children of the Kingdom while at the same time preparing to live in the world around them. This community is not perfect, but it is part of the life of discipleship. Christians coming together in worship is a strange, blessed, and wonderful thing.

Worship Is Weird

Take a moment to think about a worship service. Peer in through the stained glass windows. Whether the church is filled with the smoky fragrance of incense with an organ thrum that reaches the depths of your bones or has guitar-driven singing that accentuates the voices of the congregation, from the outside in, worship looks weird. In its High Church forms, it can appear out of step in time, an echo of ancient traditions that run counter to the LED-lit world surrounding it. Modern worship bands and a pastor in jeans and a collared shirt appear to be leading a weekly sing-along, inviting others to join with rhythms they may not know. Worship is weird. It is weird to take time each week to chant along with a pastor as his voice bellows in the nave. It is weird to join in with a song, music blasting and lyrics lit on a screen; all that's missing is the bouncing ball. This speaks nothing to the strange, mystical elements of a pastor declaring that he, as an "ordained servant of the Word," gives you forgiveness, or the fact that there will be an invitation to join in eating flesh and drinking blood.

But it's not the trappings that make worship weird—the leaders' robes, the words that are spoken, the songs that are sung, or the drone of a congregation responding in unison to certain prompts. It is weird because the Creator of the universe has come to be gathered among His people. It is the kingdom of God coming near. Gathered worship is a small glimpse of the new heavens and new earth that is to come. Through a liturgy of the promises of Jesus, the united people of God come to receive the blessings of His work over and over again. It is not about life change, though lives are changed. It is not about gaining wealth, although its practitioners are blessed. It is not about gaining favor in the sight of God, though there is peace found in that relationship. Worship is about God knowing the hearts of His creation. He knows that humanity is fickle and foolish, as the old hymn goes: "Prone to wander, Lord, I feel it; Prone to leave the God I love" (*Lutheran Service Book* 686:3). In His power, authority, majesty, and might, God could simply look down at humankind and shrug His shoulders, shake His head, and leave us to our own devices. Worse, He could dole out the justice we deserve. Instead, He brings us a rhythm of refreshment, a routine of joining together with other weary travelers to come back to His promises time and again. Worship is part of the steadfast love that God has for us. Worship is weird because this type of love is supernatural and strange. It feels alien to our hearts, which desire it yet reject it at the same time.

Embracing the Weird

Embracing the weirdness of gathered worship is important in the life of a disciple. The writer of Hebrews reminds us:

> Therefore, brothers, since we have confidence to enter the holy places by the blood of Jesus, by the new and living way that He opened for us through the curtain, that is, through His flesh, and since we have a great priest over the house of God, let us draw near with a true heart in full assurance of faith, with our hearts sprinkled clean from an evil conscience and our bodies washed with pure water. Let us hold fast the confession of our hope without wavering, for He who promised is faithful. And let us consider how to stir up one another to love and good works, not neglecting to meet together, as is the habit of some, but encouraging one another, and all the more as you see the Day drawing near. (Hebrews 10:19–25)

Here, the writer refers to "the new and living way that He opened for us through the curtain." First in the tabernacle, the traveling place of worship while the Israelites wandered in the wilderness, and then at the temple in Jerusalem, the Most Holy Place was separated from the rest of the temple by a large and heavy curtain. Think of the type of curtain you might find at a premier theater on Broadway. Behind this barrier dwelt the

Spirit of God, separated from His people. Only a priest could enter behind this border between Creator and creation. Even so, the priest would have a rope attached to his ankle and bells tied to his garments in case the presence of God so overwhelmed him that he fainted or, worse, died and needed to be pulled out. Otherwise, entering the Most Holy Place was impossible. But on the night Jesus died, "the curtain of the temple was torn in two, from top to bottom" (Matthew 27:51). The curtain is torn because the Spirit of God came out from the temple. He is going out to live among His people. This new and living way through the curtain was made by Jesus' death for us. "Do you not know that you are God's temple and that God's Spirit dwells in you?" (1 Corinthians 3:16).

Because we are temples of God, joining together in regular worship is important. Temptation abounds for disciples to see the faults of the institutional church and think, "Why do I need to gather with those people?" We are also tempted to pull worship into the realms of man-made ritual or crowd-pleasing concert. We should never turn a blind eye to the fact that in their desire for good order, people of God have done things to hold on to power over promise and purity over Gospel. The enemy will always find ways to give the Bride of Christ a black eye. But that does not negate the importance of coming together in worship.

The passage from Hebrews above ends with this exhortation: "And let us consider how to stir up one another to love and good works, not neglecting to meet together, as is the habit of some, but encouraging one another, and all the more as you see the Day drawing near" (vv. 24–25). The gathering, meeting together, is designed to stir up one another to love and good works. And it is directly connected to the fact that disciples are now temples of the living God! Embracing the weirdness of the weekly worship gathering is about how God refills us! He knows humanity's struggles; He knows the temptations of the shiny things of this world; He knows the exhaustion that would set in on the discipleship journey. As the Giver of all good gifts, He gave us worship in all its weird and supernatural glory. A time set aside for fellow travelers to rest in the promises of Jesus and to be called to love and good works! A time when personal sinfulness may be set directly in front of gazing eyes, but that would immediately be followed with the blessing of the assurances of grace. Songs that declare the promises of God in a way that locks them into our heads so they may pass to our hearts and move out into our hands. A liturgy that shows the worshipers the reality of their lives and continually points back to Jesus and what He has done for them. Worshiping together, embracing the weirdness, reminds us that God did not leave us alone. His promises are found in the places of faith, where we hope but cannot always see, but they also find physical expression in the gift of His Body gathered in worship.

The Blessings of Gathered Worship

Establishing the fact that worship comes from a strange supernatural place is important, but how exactly do the promises of God work out into our lives? Breaking down pieces of a worship service will give us insight into how gathering together is more than simply joining a weekly ritual of song and tradition. All types of Christian worship have some form of liturgy or system they follow. Confessions, prayer, singing, preaching, and celebration of Baptism and the Lord's Supper happen as key forms of all types of worship practice. Within the Lutheran world, our liturgy revolves around the Gospel as given to us through the Word of God. Psalms, Scripture readings, hymns, spiritual songs, prayers, liturgical elements, preaching, and Sacraments all center on the work of Jesus on the cross for us. Each of these pieces of worship is built intentionally to be a part of the life of discipleship. Some of these elements are instituted by God; others are gifts of God used by His people to bring hearts and minds back to Him. As these components of worship come together, all blessed by the Lord, they work to build up believers in faith and help them respond to what Jesus has done for them.

Song

Singing in worship, especially gathered worship, is a strange, strange thing. At a choir concert, the audience sits back and enjoys a combination of melody and harmony woven together by the musicians onstage. At a pop or rock concert, there are no lyrics for the crowd, yet many know them and sing along, dancing as they do. Whether music is meant to be participatory or not, rarely does our culture come together around music in such a way as happens in the worship service. From hymnals to screens, there are many songs available for churches to use as they gather. But why is song such an important part of worship and therefore for the life of the disciple?

First and foremost, singing is a scriptural act praised throughout the Bible:

- He put a new song in my mouth, a song of praise to our God. Many will see and fear, and put their trust in the LORD. (Psalm 40:3)

- Oh sing to the LORD a new song; sing to the LORD, all the earth! (Psalm 96:1)

- Oh sing to the LORD a new song, for He has done marvelous things! His right hand and His holy arm have worked salvation for Him. (Psalm 98:1)

- Sing to the LORD a new song, His praise from the end of the earth, you who go down to the sea, and all that fills it, the coastlands and their inhabitants. (Isaiah 42:10)

- Be filled with the Spirit, addressing one another in psalms and hymns and spiritual songs, singing and making melody to the Lord with your heart. (Ephesians 5:18–19)

- And they sang a new song, saying, "Worthy are You to take the scroll and to open its seals, for You were slain, and by Your blood You ransomed people for God from every tribe and language and people and nation, and You have made them a kingdom and priests to our God, and they shall reign on the earth." (Revelation 5:9–10)

Song is a theme in Scripture. Rarely, if ever, is a gathered worship service of God's people absent some form of singing. From the days of Abraham until now, song has been a key part of worship. Moses composed a song of praise after God defeated the Egyptians at the Red Sea (Exodus 15:1–8). David was brought into the tents of Saul to calm the king with his ballads and then went on to author and commission the Psalms, the greatest hymnbook of the faith. Right after instituting the Lord's Supper and right before His betrayal, Jesus joined His disciples in a hymn (Matthew 26:30). The writers of the many epistles of the New Testament encouraged the saints to sing as a form of worship. Finally, the Church gathered in the new heavens and new earth will sing to and of the Lamb who was slain for the world. Throughout Scripture, song is used to proclaim the promises of God, to declare His glory, and to rejoice in His steadfast love. It is a language that speaks to the head, heart, and hands of disciples.

HEAD

While everyone knows me as Ted, my given name is Theodore. I truly enjoy that my parents gave me that name, even though people immediately asked if I was friends with Alvin and Simon when I told them my name growing up. When I was a kid, Theodore was a tough name to spell. On one of our cross-country trips from Texas to Minnesota to visit grandparents, my dad sat down next to me at lunch at a rest stop. My mom and brother and sister were packing away the lunch we had just eaten, putting things into our red Coleman cooler. As Dad sat down, he placed a yellow package of peanut M&M's on the table, my favorite candy even to this day. He looked at me and said, "Ted, I want to teach you a song." Using a melody and lyrics of his own creation, Dad sang to me, "T-H-E-O-D-O-R, E, that's me, The-o-dore." He had me learn it as we sat there on the bench of the picnic table. Then he said, "If you can learn it and sing it back to me, this bag of M&M's is yours." I don't know if he ever regretted it, but I sang that song for the next hour as I ate my M&M's. When I have to sign my full name on any document for legal reasons, I catch myself singing or humming the song. It's a simple song my dad wrote on a cross-country road trip, but the lesson continues today. That is the power of song.

Singing takes words, puts them to a melody, and writes them in our brain. Students have used song to memorize states, dates, and books of the Bible. For the disciple, song carries with it an important power: it takes the promises of Jesus and ingrains them in our minds. When I was scared as a child, my mom would sing me the hymn "God Loves Me Dearly." When trouble comes, when I am facing anxiety and the unknown, this promise through song is ingrained in me:

> God loves me dearly, Grants me salvation,
> God loves me dearly, Loves even me.
> Therefore I'll say again: God loves me dearly,
> God loves me dearly, Loves even me.
>
> He sent forth Jesus, My dear Redeemer,
> He sent forth Jesus And set me free.
> Therefore I'll say again: God loves me dearly,
> God loves me dearly, Loves even me.
> (*Lutheran Service Book* 392:1, 3)

The power in those words! Steadfast love declared again and again. Simple tune, simple lyrics, timeless truth. In the discipleship journey, song brings us back to the promises of Jesus. It calls us to Him. Song is one of the most powerful everyday tools of the disciple. Need to come back and return to the promises of salvation again? Remember the words of "Amazing Grace." Feeling alone and lost on this journey, and wondering if there is any help? Let the words of "Abide with Me" give voice to those feelings and return you to the hope of Jesus. There is an incredible list of songs that are cornerstones for disciples as they walk this journey. Do not neglect song! It is a powerful tool for memory and trusting in the promises of Jesus.

Scripture exhorts disciples to proclaim, declare, and sing the glory of God. Song blesses the knowledge of disciples because it reminds them of this key aspect of faith: God is God. It may seem strange to say that, but songs declare the great work of God. Psalm 105:2 encourages disciples to "sing to Him, sing praises to Him; tell of all His wondrous works!" But why? If God doesn't need His followers to fill His "God battery," why should we sing of how great He is? Because it reminds disciples of that fact. It brings into sharp contrast the likes of humanity with their Creator. It once again teaches the promises of God: He is Creator, He is mightier, He is to be feared. Yet, He comes to us with steadfast love and gives His Son for the sake of His creation.

HEART

Song can also transform the heart of the disciple. The head knowledge of what songs deliver is important, but the gift of song does not end there. With the connection of head to heart, the gift of song affects the soul.

Many Christian people have a favorite hymn or song they sing when their community gathers. Some may be connected to a season: a joyful, candlelit "Silent Night" on Christmas Eve; the somber tones of "Go to Dark Gethsemane" on Good Friday; the triumphant notes of trumpets joining in on "I Know That My Redeemer Lives" on Easter! Music moves the soul. It is a strange thing and incredibly supernatural. Song has the ability to lift us out of foul moods, to create joy or solemn contemplation. In worship, song is not a tool to manipulate emotion but a gift to connect the head and the heart.

Whether the song was written long ago or yesterday, there is incredible blessing in how music can drive the promises of Jesus into the soul of the disciple. Ancient hymns and modern praise are built for disciples to not only know the promises of Jesus but also feel them actively at work in their lives. Comfort, joy, and peace can be found in songs created to deliver the promises of Jesus to His people.

Song assists in filling up the disciple for the journey. A side blessing of song when it bridges the head and the heart is that it fills and restores the soul. This is done best when connected to the full gathered worship service, but throughout history, disciples have used psalms, hymns, and spiritual songs to abide in and be filled by the promises of Jesus throughout the journey. Joining together in song with the assembled family of God blesses them with a rejuvenation and restoration of body and mind.

HANDS

Now, one important thing was skipped in discussing song in the life of worship. It is—and hold on to your hats for this reveal—important to actually *sing*. While this might seem obvious, there can be many fears around singing. Self-consciousness can sneak in to ruin a beautiful gift. This doesn't mean you have to be in the choir, but the act of singing is an important part of song in worship. Singing, actually vocalizing the song, takes the promises of Jesus found in song and completes the head, heart, and hands connection.

Singing is confessional. Paul states this in his Letter to the Church in Rome:

> "The word is near you, in your mouth and in your heart" (that is, the word of faith that we proclaim); because, if you confess with your mouth that Jesus is Lord and believe in your heart that God raised Him from the dead, you will be saved. For with the heart one believes and is justified, and with the mouth one confesses and is saved. (10:8–10)

The promises sung are a confession of faith. They state who Jesus is, the promises He keeps, and who you are because of them. This simple act takes song to the realm of action, from head to heart to hands. It is a beautiful physical expression of inner belief and confession.

Discipleship is not lived alone, and there is always opportunity to be an example to others in the faith. What does the young father learn from the white-haired elder who belts out the hymns on a Sunday morning? How about the teenager who watches a favorite Sunday School teacher sing with gusto? Discipleship is lived in simple ways. Singing together as gathered people of God gives example, expression, and permission for those who seek to grow in their faith. What a seemingly ordinary gift with extraordinary potential!

If there is still a fear of how one sounds in the midst of worship, just remember with a laugh that the Lord said to make a joyful *noise*—He didn't say it had to be perfect.

Confession and Absolution

Disciples need this reminder: confession is key in the journey. Too often there is a mistaken belief that followers of Jesus need to be perfect. Founded in works-based righteousness, this is false. (It is a lie whispered by the devil into the ears of believers to discourage them.) When disciples believe this lie, it has an effect on their witness to the unbelieving world as well. As Christians try to live life in perfect accord and yet fail time and again, they then push their anger outward, onto the "heathens" and "pagans." No longer is the lost sheep seen wandering in the darkness in need of the light of Gospel. No, the battle has moved away from powers and principalities to a war on those who would not believe as Christians do. Worship has a powerful weapon against this falsehood: Confession and Absolution.

As part of their time gathered together, disciples confess their sins. Public confession in worship does not require you to declare your specific sins of the week from your seat in the sanctuary. Instead, it sets aside time for the people of God to admit sin together. This could be misconstrued as a time when the Church tears itself down. How could anyone possibly want to join a community where, on a weekly basis, the people look over their failure purposely? where time is spent bringing to mind things that have gone wrong? This is not some form of self-flagellation. In fact, it is a command of Scripture: "If we say we have no sin, we deceive ourselves, and the truth is not in us" (1 John 1:8). Being aware of sinfulness is an important part of discipleship. Our journey through life trusting, seeking, and following Jesus will not be without personal and moral failures—times when we travelers find ourselves doing exactly what we had hoped not to do. Confession puts all the cards on the table. Nothing is hidden. Instead, this time set aside in worship reinforces the fact that Christians are imperfect people in need of a perfect Savior.

Confession is never left alone; it is always followed immediately by absolution. Listen to what comes directly after the verse quoted above: "If we confess our sins, He is faithful and just to forgive us our sins and to cleanse us from all unrighteousness" (1 John 1:9). The Good News of Jesus' promises is delivered after confession. The absolution of sin is another beautiful gift of worship, a declaration of the work of God on behalf of His people. Confession and Absolution is not a time to look inward and say, "Oh, woe is me, I am a terrible sinner!" Instead, it is a time of wonderful fulfillment of promise. Jesus' words come alive. It is proof not of how weak the person is, but of how powerful the Savior.

Joining together in public Confession and Absolution builds the Body of Christ together. It strengthens every disciple who is present. No one enjoys feeling alone, as if they are the only screwup. But together in Confession and Absolution, a group of people admit their faults and failures. They hear God once again prove His steadfast love. Forgiveness is proclaimed over them. This takes disciples back to the source. It is the never-ending spring bubbling up from the ground, building to the river of life, freeing and refreshing disciples. It acknowledges that we can't deny the reality of failure on this journey. Instead, that reality proves once again how good God is along the way.)

The Rhythms of Worship

Joining together in worship is part of being a disciple. But that does not mean that worship is contained to one day a week. There is an ebb and flow of worship throughout the week. Each day should contain moments for the disciple to slow down and worship. Many of the acts of worship are daily available to the disciple, smaller moments to rest and refuel. They do not replace the gathering of the Church together. But they are still a blessing.

Singing during the week can continue to reinforce the head, heart, and hands connection of Jesus' promises. One of the brilliant things about the Internet is that the whole of worship-based music is just a click away. Yard work, dishes, or cleaning can become a time of worship in song. Simply find the music you are looking for and sing along.

Confession and Absolution brings the promises of God to those gathered in worship; however, they don't end at the door of the church building. "Therefore, confess your sins to one another and pray for one another" (James 5:16). There is opportunity throughout the week. Parents to children, with children learning to forgive their parents. Friends can model this with friends. Husbands to wives, wives to husbands. Bosses to employees. Teachers to students. Confession and Absolution together in worship is important, but it's something we do in everyday life as well. Private Confession and Absolution with a pastor is also an incredible gift—a time set aside to come and confess out loud sins committed and specifically hear the words of absolution from the pastor.

Worship happens while people are gathered together. But it is also important to have moments of worship throughout the week.

Worship should not always be a solitary activity for those on the journey of discipleship. It is to be joined in with others as a band of people called together under the promises of Jesus. It may feel strange and supernatural, but that's because it is. God is delivering His gifts through worship. It is a blessing. Christians need not try to make God happy through their worship. Instead, He gives gifts to them. Through song, Confession and Absolution, and the gathering together of God's people, the disciple's journey continues forward.

As if that were not enough, God physically brings gifts and promises to His people. This simple, weekly time is punctuated by God breaking into His creation to deliver His grace. But more on that in the next chapter.

OPEN WITH PRAYER

Ask for a volunteer to open with prayer. Rotate who does this each time you get together. Praying in front of people may scare you, but it is worth growing in the practice. Praying together is part of what the Body of Christ does. Not only is it our connection to God but it also gives an example of how we live on this discipleship journey.

FROM LAST TIME

How did it go, keeping an eye out for bad fruit? What happened when you stopped and abided, using Psalm 23 and prayer? What were your experiences?

DISCUSSION

1. What jumped out to you in this chapter?

2. Have you ever been the good kind of lost—your directions took you a different route, but it was worth it?

3. Is there anything about worship that you find weird? What is it?

4. What is your favorite song sung at church?

5. Are there any church songs that connect your head, heart, and hands? What are they? How do they do that?

6. How does Confession and Absolution affect you during worship?

DO IT

Go to church. Join in with the gathered believers and let the Lord serve you in that time. Pick out one thing from this week that helped you grow during the worship service. Be prepared to share it with the group next time.

Bonus: Get involved! Ask leaders at your church how you can volunteer to help on Sundays. Don't just be a participant in the pews; be a part of the team! Double bonus if the group reading this together is from the same church and asks to volunteer as a unit.

CLOSING

Make sure you know when you are getting together next.

Pray for one another. Take prayer requests and close in prayer. Spread out the prayer requests so as many people are praying as are available.

BEFORE NEXT TIME

Read chapter 4, prepare answers for the questions, and be prepared to share how worship affected you.

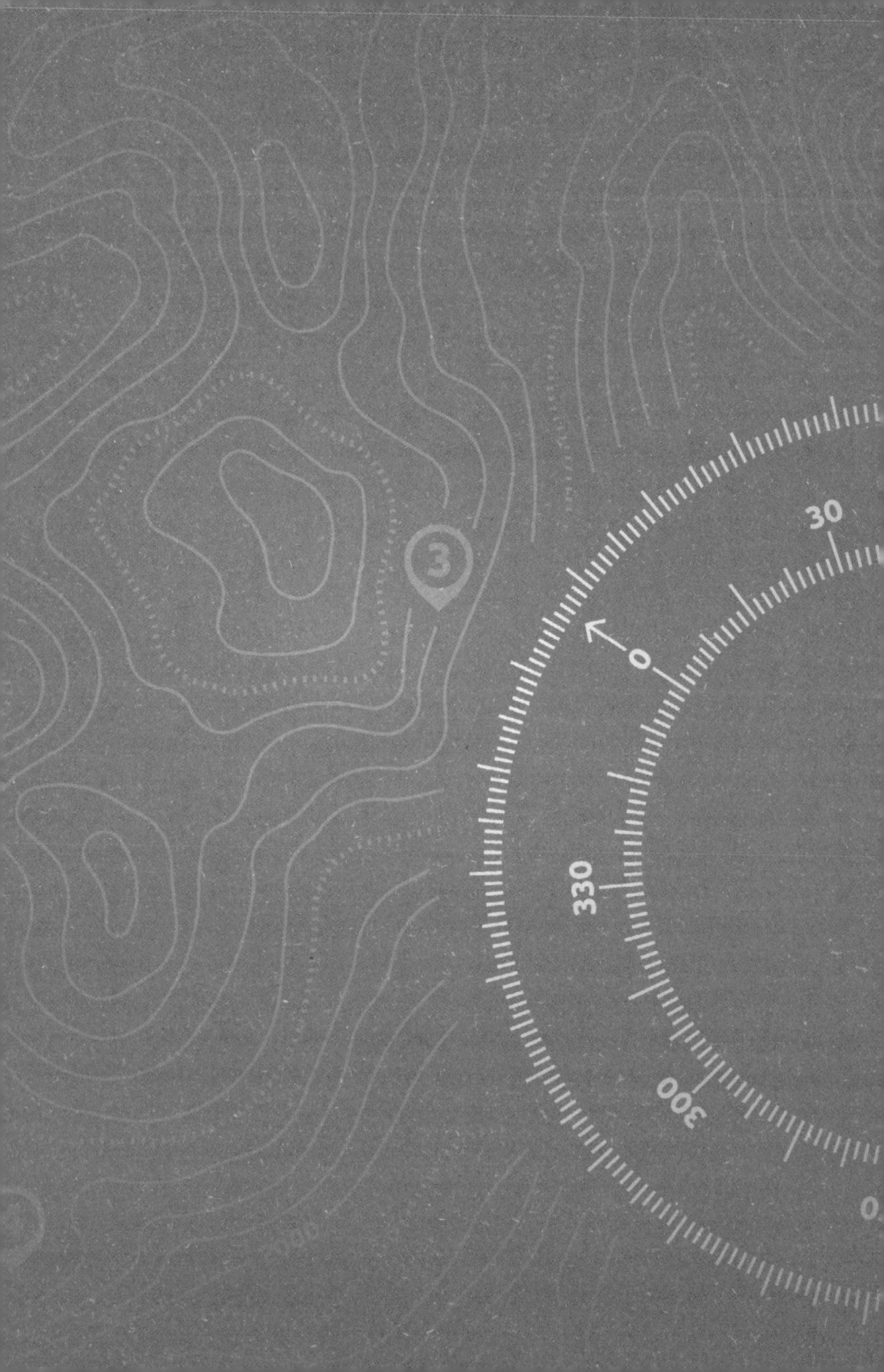
3
30
0
330
300

Word and Sacrament Renewal

There is an old heresy that often grabs hold at the heart of humanity. It claims that the spiritual is superior to the physical. It whispers of a secret knowledge that must be attained by practitioners of the faith. Books have been written and movies made around its outlandish tenets because it has all the dogma of works-righteousness with the trappings of a conspiracy theory. This belief system is called Gnosticism,[1] and the Early Church battled it many times.

A type of Gnosticism has worked its way into American Christianity. In this idea, once again, the spiritual is greater than the physical—spiritual acuity and prowess are raised above the works of the physical world. Heaven is a place where the saints ascend when they have died, from which to look down upon the world below. Discipleship is not about trusting, seeking, and following but is instead a series of secret texts and tomes that lead to a transformed mind-set, open only to a select few. In this system, the disciple is constantly looking for the next bit of secret knowledge in order to grow. The Church becomes a caste system where those who have attained a higher level of spiritual knowledge look down upon the lowly who do not have the ability to gain that hidden insight.

---

1   Pronounced "NOSS-ti-sizm"—the *G* is silent.

This may sound like a cult, but look at your own life. Are there places where you feel like you have a higher level of understanding of God? Do you look down on others because they are not as learned as you? Seeking God is an important part of discipleship, but the old heresy can slowly creep in when we try to seek God apart from where He promises to be found. Seeking God never distances itself from the real and tangible gifts that God has given. The old Gnostic ways claimed that a lower deity created the physical world, and thus it was lesser and even evil. Fallacies created by this way of thinking mean that to attain a spiritual enlightenment, one must find and possess a secret knowledge of God and the world. The confession of the Christian Church is that God created everything. Spiritual and physical, He created it all. At the end of each day of creation, He looked around and said it is good. When was the last time you made seven pancakes on a Saturday morning and thought to yourself, "These are all good pancakes"? Looking at what you create and claiming it is good can be hard. Yet, God looks down at the earth, the seas, the stars, the moon, the creatures, and humanity and has a simple response: He made it good. Even after sin corrupted that creation, God in His steadfast love did not destroy that which was fallen but instead decided to save it. The knowledge of God is spiritual and physical, laid out for His people. God does not hide His ways from His people; rather, He gifts it to His people and it is good.

When disciples trust the ways of Jesus, they don't need secret knowledge. They don't need to search out vast realms or Indiana Jones their way into a mysterious library. No. They have a physical gift from God for their benefit: His Word and Sacraments. God has continually worked His justice and mercy on this world through physical, created means. Here are some examples.

Moses' Calling

God called Moses through a burning bush. A burning bush. Not even a large tree, just some random shrubbery. He could have used something more noble or simply lit up the sky with a giant, God-style Bat signal. Instead, He used a simple bush and supernatural fire. Spiritual and physical. But God wasn't done there. Moses expressed his concern that he wouldn't be the right person for the job—he's not a good public speaker, and how will anyone believe him?

> Then Moses answered, "But behold, they will not believe me or listen to my voice, for they will say, 'The LORD did not appear to you.'" The LORD said to him, "What is that in your hand?" He said, "A staff." And He said, "Throw it on the ground." So he threw it on the ground, and it became a serpent, and Moses ran from it. But the LORD said to Moses, "Put out your hand and catch it by the tail"—so he put out his hand and caught it, and it became a staff in his hand—"that they may believe that the LORD, the God of their fathers, the God of Abraham, the God of Isaac, and the God of Jacob, has appeared to you." (Exodus 4:1–5)

Moses is worried, and God reassures him by basically saying, "Oh, good point. So you've got that stick; watch what I can do." Physical and spiritual. Creation and divine.

Touching Jesus' Robe

In Luke 8, a woman who is suffering an extreme flow of blood finds her last hope in seeking out Jesus. The crowds surround Him, but her hope is that she can reach out and just touch a corner on His garment. Throughout the Old Testament, there are references to wings and their protection and healing. Malachi 4:2, for example: "But for you who fear My name, the sun of righteousness shall rise with healing in its wings." This woman knew the stories of the Messiah and His power. If only she could touch that corner of His garment, that wing, then surely she would be healed. When she does, this is what happens:

> She came up behind Him and touched the fringe of His garment, and immediately her discharge of blood ceased. And Jesus said, "Who was it that touched Me?" When all denied it, Peter said, "Master, the crowds surround You and are pressing in on You!" But Jesus said, "Someone touched Me, for I perceive that power has gone out from Me." And when the woman saw that she was not hidden, she came trembling, and falling down before Him declared in the presence of all the people why she had touched Him, and how she had been immediately healed. And He said to her, "Daughter, your faith has made you well; go in peace." (Luke 8:44–48)

The edge of a robe and a faith that trusted the promises of God. Once again, a simple garment and a supernatural trust that what God said is what He meant. Look at how Jesus responds: "Daughter, your faith has made you well; go in peace."

She didn't try to meditate her way into some new healing powers. Desperate, she simply reached out to touch Jesus.

God provides for His people. He knows us. He knows that we are people made of spiritual and physical, both parts created to work in concert together. Because of this, He gives disciples gifts that encompass both the physical and spiritual. These gifts are not the identity of a disciple but rather touchstones that bring the disciple back to that promised identity.

The path of discipleship does not exist in some ethereal realm. More often than not, discipleship looks like coffee on a Monday morning, not an enlightened meditation surrounded by candles and contemplation of the minutiae of spirituality. A simple life of discipleship takes place as feet hit the ground out of bed, as the mundane tasks of the day are taken care of, and after slipping under the covers at night. Push away the idea that you might be unworthy as a disciple because you cannot attain some higher spiritual plane. Look at the original people who followed Jesus. They were tax collectors and fishermen, prostitutes and housewives. They came from all different walks of life but had one thing in common: they followed Jesus. Do not fall into the belief that the only way to grow as a disciple is by gaining or attaining knowledge of the path. Growth in discipleship comes from walking the path daily, from baby steps to sprints and everything in between. The act of living as a disciple is what makes a disciple. The promises of Jesus physically manifesting through His people are the ways of discipleship.

God not only understands that humans are both physical and spiritual; He actually created us to be that way. He created our physical bodies and then gave life with His own breath:

"Then the LORD God formed the man of dust from the ground and breathed into his nostrils the breath of life, and the man became a living creature" (Genesis 2:7). Dirt and breath. Physical and spiritual. God knows His people cannot have only one or the other. Because of this, He works physical and spiritual together to care for us, giving gifts knitted in both the everyday and the supernatural to benefit His people.

Word

Selling 3.9 billion copies in a span of only fifty years, the Bible outmatched the next best-selling book by 3.08 billion.[2] Let that sink in. Enough physical copies of the Bible are sold for half the population of the earth. The Word of God has gone out mightily. But how often is it just collecting dust on your nightstand?

For a moment, indulge in a cliché about the Bible that corresponds to the metaphor of hiking through the mountains. In this scenario, the Bible is the map for the disciple. Within its bindings, or the soft illuminations of a smartphone, are the guiding principles, keys, elevation lines, marked paths, and overview for the disciple's journey. It will show the way when lost and guide a path through the woods. The mapmaker has taken the time to mark down the trail; the explorer need only follow it.

Journeying as a disciple must include this map. The Bible, the Word of God, is one of the chief gifts given by God. While at times it may confuse or confound, within its pages God speaks to His people. He gives them the truth about the created order.

---

2   Jennifer Polland, "The 10 Most Read Books in the World," *Business Insider*, December 27, 2012, https://www.businessinsider.com/the-top-10-most-read-books-in-the-world-infographic -2012-12.

Stories within can be held up as examples for what are and what are not the ways of God. As the author of Hebrews exhorts, "The word of God is living and active, sharper than any two-edged sword, piercing to the division of soul and of spirit, of joints and of marrow, and discerning the thoughts and intentions of the heart" (4:12). Being a disciple means being in the Word of God. Just as the hiker could easily become lost without a map, so, too, can the disciple who neglects the Word.

This may seem like a simple idea. Of course a disciple would read the Bible! Yet, often in life it is the simple things that we end up neglecting. How does a baseball player win a Gold Glove? He takes grounder after grounder in practice. How does the master artist paint her masterpiece? She paints smaller paintings every day, building her skill as she matures. A disciple following after Jesus does not come out fully formed. It is an art, a practice, an everyday return to the promises of God. But what an incredible gift! Simple pages in a book; God telling His story to His people. Physical and spiritual. A means through which God communicates. Banish from your mind the idea that you need a burning bush or a multitude of angels. Though God will work how He may, He has physically placed in your hands His Word—His map for your journey of discipleship.

Rooted in the Word

Therefore, as you received Christ Jesus the Lord, so walk in Him, rooted and built up in Him and established in the faith, just as you were taught, abounding in thanksgiving. (Colossians 2:6–7)

Limestone and hard-packed dirt make up the yard of the Central Texas house where we currently live. The design of our neighborhood makes it hard to notice that we sit on the top of a hill. Before being sold to a developer, it was simply grazing land. The dirt was too rocky and tough to plant any crops, and the low-lying junipers would be hard to clear without a team of bulldozers. One night a strong wind blew through the neighborhood, the rain right behind it. I stood in the windows of our upstairs landing, fretting as I watched our two small trees sway. These trees *had* to make it! Someday they would be the large shade trees we so desired, but at barely three inches around and ten to fifteen feet tall, they looked like they might lose this round to the wind. I rushed out and was quickly soaked by the rain as I drove some stakes into the ground and used ratchet straps to brace the trees.

The next day, I stood on my front driveway staring at the trees, trying to formulate a plan. A next-door neighbor came over, and we started talking about the trees and how it had looked as if they would be uprooted the night before. He mentioned that with the state of our soil and the speed at which the neighborhood had been constructed, there was a possibility these trees had built up root balls. Instead of the roots delving deeply into the ground, they had been forced in on themselves by the hard dirt, rocks, and method of planting. The balled roots could hold the trees against some wind, but it was likely that at some point they would be blown over.

Disciples root themselves in the Word of God because they know the storms will come. The winds will blow, guaranteed. The enemy will seek to destroy. Remember, it is one of the promises of Jesus (John 16:33). Being rooted in the Word is about attaching to the source, the promises of Jesus. These promises are found and clearly spelled out in the Word of God. God uses this simple means to deliver the promises to His people. Sinking roots down into the good soil and fresh springs of the Bible strengthens the disciple.

Saying you are rooted in the Word of God is a great thing. It is poetic and paints an image for our minds to see, but it cannot live solely in the realm of theory. What if a hiker had a map and loved the idea of what the map stood for, but never pulled it out? The Word of God is meant to be used in the personal journey of disciples, among a community on the path together, and to be heard in the midst of trusting, seeking, and following.

A Personal Word

Hear, O Israel: The LORD our God, the LORD is one. You shall love the LORD your God with all your heart and with all your soul and with all your might. And these words that I command you today shall be on your heart. You shall teach them diligently to your children, and shall talk of them when you sit in your house, and when you walk by the way, and when you lie down, and when you rise. You shall bind them as a sign on your hand, and they shall be as frontlets between your eyes. You shall write them on the doorposts of your house and on your gates. (Deuteronomy 6:4–9)

A disciple's Bible should never be far from reach, whether it is an old copy received as a gift, one picked out from the shelf personally, or an app on the nearest device. The Word of God should be easily and quickly accessible.

One's Bible should be quickly accessible because it should be frequently used. Devotionals, quiet time, journaling—these are a few of the many ways that one can spend personal time in the Word. A time set aside for study and reflection. A meaningful personal walk in the Word is foundational for the journey of discipleship. In this time, the disciple is laid bare. Personal sin is never more revealed, yet the Savior quickly redeems. The words of the Scriptures flow into the disciple's life as roots dig deeper into the promises God has given His people. When the winds come and the storms blow, disciples are not shaken because they are anchored in the Word of God.

There are many thoughts on the when, where, and how of this time in the Word. Some would say the best time for Scripture is in the morning, right as one wakes up. Others have chosen lunch breaks, after dinner, or before bed for their time in the Word. Some lock themselves in their rooms, others splay over their kitchen tables, and some put on their headphones while pulling up their Bible app at their favorite coffee shop. Is a devotional book necessary? Journaling your thoughts and questions seems to be a good idea. All of these things are good. But the most important thing? Spending time in the Word. Find what works best for you. Push away things that would distract you. If you don't function well until after you have had your coffee, brew it as you pull out your Bible. Do you enjoy the framework of a good devotional? Make sure you have one. There will be many temptations to set aside Scripture for seemingly more urgent things. Instead, work out a way to make God's Word a priority.

The Word Spoken

So faith comes from hearing, and hearing through the word of Christ. (Romans 10:17)

Now it is important to recognize another aspect of the Word at work in the life of the disciple: the spoken Word. Preaching is a biblical model of how the Word is brought to the people of God. In the physical act of the Word being spoken and heard, the Holy Spirit works on the head, heart, and hands. Here again is the ordinary, supernatural work of God using physical means to work in the spiritual realms. There is nothing overtly mystical about a sermon. A pastor spends time in prayer, reading, study, and presentation, but at the end of the day it is a man standing in front of people talking about the Word of God. But a promise is contained there. Faith comes by hearing. Could it have something to do with the fact that when the physical world was created, it was *spoken* into existence? that in the same way the human spirit is buoyed and refreshed by the Word spoken?

The Word does not go out without effect. God makes that promise in Scripture (Isaiah 55:10–11). This is why disciples should be paying close attention when they listen to the words of preachers. Once again, not because these men are masters of some mystical art, but because the Word of God is going out into the world in a powerful way. It will convict and encourage, tear down idols, and reinforce the foundation of the Savior.

Our enemy prowls like a lion, seeking to devour. Just look at the world surrounding you. There is sickness, disease, classism, racism, political conniving, power brokering, and all other kinds of sin. Temptation comes and says, "Just try this a little. It will be okay." A foot steps off the path. Then another. Slowly, methodically, a disciple has been pulled away from trusting, seeking, and following Jesus. Preaching is meant to be a voice calling through the wilderness. That voice reminds the disciple of the path, the goodness of walking in the ways of the Lord, and the peace of the Savior. Good preaching brings a simple message: you have failed and will continue to fail; you have a Savior; go and love God and your neighbor. It is that simple.

Disciples will welcome preaching that challenges them. There has always been a need to try to make people feel better. To look at the journey of faith and think that it must always feel good or be positive. But even Jesus did not hold to those things. Good preaching will at times feel like the stinging of a wound. Why? Because our sin leaves festering gashes in our lives. These ways that are not of God will tear us down and open us up bit by bit. The goal of our enemy is that we would not see the wounds, that they would simply blend in and be forgotten—not healed or scarred over but camouflaged as they continue to bleed. Preaching is the sting of the alcohol swab reaching the wound and making us aware of what is happening as it begins cleansing. We will be tempted to try to explain away those actions, thoughts, and feelings, to justify sinful acts. The spoken Word reveals this trickery and shows the disciples the ways in which they have walked away from God. It may be hard, but it is necessary to see the areas of life that are in need of repentance.

Disciples need the reassurance that hearing the Word of God provides. When God's Word is spoken over His people, be it in preaching, reading Scripture, or Confession and Absolution, it brings with it the deep, cool, rejuvenating springs of the Gospel. Not only that, but it is the Gospel for *you*. This is not some theoretical idea or theological discussion. The Gospel speaks of a real Savior who constantly brings forgiveness and grace to His people in need. It is the foundation. Disciples should lock in and listen for this on a constant basis. The Word of God spoken for them will be direct and powerful.

When preaching brings the force of the Law and the power of the Gospel, it leads to a rejuvenated disciple who lives to trust, seek, and follow. Preaching that convicts and then reassures delivers the promises of Jesus in the lives of disciples. The Word of God calls people to more. This Word is spoken into the hearers' lives as they do the work of loving God and loving others. This is why the Church, for all its faults, has been known for the good it has done. In a world that seeks secular idols and false prophets from all corners of theology and philosophy, good preaching calls on the redeemed people of God to go out into the places they live and be salt and light, actively proclaiming the promises of Jesus.

Sacrament

God also uses His Word united with the physical as a gift in the lives of His disciples. We call that interaction between the Word and the world a sacrament—that mysterious, beautiful meeting place where created elements take on spiritual importance. Baptism and the Lord's Supper are gifts from God that demonstrate His tangible grace.

Journeying as a disciple will take its toll. There will be days filled with wonder and days of weariness. In the darkest moments, disciples will ask themselves, "I see what I have done and how I have wondered, could I possibly be saved?" The Word of God responds time and again with a profound "Yes!" But God, knowing His people, does not stop there. He continues to give perfect gifts. In the Sacraments, God places His promises in the hands of His people.

Baptism

> Baptism, which corresponds to this, now saves you, not as a removal of dirt from the body but as an appeal to God for a good conscience, through the resurrection of Jesus Christ. (1 Peter 3:21)

Simple water connected with the Word of God is a cleansing fire and the steadfast love of God made real. Baptism is the promise of Jesus drowning all the sin that would keep you up late at night. It is a definitive answer to the question of salvation. The waters of Baptism call disciples back to their identity in Christ. Familial bonds of the Church emerge from the waters as the trinitarian authority over sin is proclaimed. Disciples do not have to hunt for the spring of life; Jesus picks it up and brings it to them.

Live in the daily reality of your Baptism. The promise of Jesus is actively with you. In your Baptism, God reached down and took hold of you, and He will not let you go. When the world comes crashing down or when the enemy is on the hunt, your Baptism lays claim to who and whose you are. In a life of discipleship, we will struggle with losing track of our identity.

There will be many things that seek to step in and tell you what makes you, you. Baptism lays hold of that claim and will not let it be wrestled away.

Return to your Baptism. It is such a simple thing. For many disciples, it may happen when they are infants, before they can even have memory of it. But Baptism is a physical assurance of a spiritual reality. Make it a part of prayer, of your study of the Word, and of conversation. Rely on it as the powerful sacrament that it is. Take time to remember when you wash your hands, take a shower, or go swimming. Add a spiritual discipline to it. On your baptismal birthday, celebrate what the Lord has done! Let the God who created the rushing streams and mighty oceans use His creation to reassure you of the promise that was delivered to you long ago. Live in that reality.

The Lord's Supper

Now as they were eating, Jesus took bread, and after blessing it broke it and gave it to the disciples, and said, "Take, eat; this is My body." And He took a cup, and when He had given thanks He gave it to them, saying, "Drink of it, all of you, for this is My blood of the covenant, which is poured out for many for the forgiveness of sins." (Matthew 26:26–28)

While I was at seminary, I had to write an in-depth look at Moses striking the rock to bring water to the people of Israel. As part of the assignment, I needed to present what I planned to write about to my professor before starting my paper. In my memory, I had some fancy take on the rock and the stream and what it all meant. As I sat in my professor's office excitedly explaining my plan as he looked over my paper outline, I thought I was bringing a brand-new outlook on these verses. When I had finished, my professor looked up over my outline in his hand and said, "Why don't you write about Moses' staff?"

Moses' staff? But this was not someone to whom I wanted to say no. Thus began several weeks of me translating Scripture and then writing—and rewriting—an end-of-course capstone paper on Moses' staff. And what an incredible blessing it has become in my life. As I did a deep dive into all the miracles God worked through a stick, the Sacraments became more real to me. God has been using physical means to convey His promises since the beginning of creation. If I could believe the wonders God worked through this staff, what more could He do through bread and wine?

God knows what His people will experience. He knows that there will be trials and tribulations. But instead of looking down on His creation and His people as if they have been set in motion and can now be left to their own devices, He brings them a gift. He takes a meal that has long been known, the Passover, and places Himself in the place of the sacrifice. The beautiful mystery is that it becomes *His* Supper, not because of power and might, but because of sacrifice. This bread is now body, this wine is now blood. In this meal is forgiveness. When the question comes, "Could I possibly be forgiven?" Jesus proclaims, "Yes! See, touch, and taste how good forgiveness is!"

This meal is the promise of Jesus delivered physically to the disciple. Taking this meal together is a blessing for the Body of Christ gathered together. This beautiful mystery blesses the disciple.

God provides in physical ways. Whether it is the Bible sitting on your nightstand, the latest sermon from your pastor, the waters of your Baptism, or the most recent time you took the Lord's Supper, He brings His gifts directly to you. Any idol that would draw attention away from the journey of discipleship tries to offer either physical euphoria or spiritual distraction. But neither provides the promises present when God uses His created means as a delivery method. Each of these gifts—the Word read and spoken, Baptism, and the Lord's Supper—brings blessing to the disciple. It is not about some secret knowledge but instead about a God who would use physical creation to bring spiritual blessing.

Word and Sacrament bring renewal. It is as simple as that. They bring the disciple back to the promises of Jesus through physical means. It would be easy to get lost in a transformation that would focus on knowing more about God or finding that one secret thing that will bring about your destiny. Instead, God uses plain, simple things to provide for His people. Do not buy into the idea that some ethereal spiritual destiny is right around the corner if it can only be reached or that the journey's struggles will end quickly. Instead, hold out for these promises, these beautiful mysteries, where God blesses His people through creation for their benefit.

Slow down. Receive these blessings. Let them renew you. This renewal is not of yourself but instead is a gift of God. It would be easy to underestimate these simple things. Yet, God uses simple things. Discipleship, while not a sacrament, is another physical manifestation of spiritual realities. God is working in your life. In the exciting and the mundane, in the expected and the unexpected, at the home, office, and neighborhood, God is at work through His people. God works through physical means. Just look at the work that Jesus did while He was present on the earth, physically walking among God's creation. The physical and spiritual were created to intermingle. As disciples, we work through this in our daily lives. We trust the promises of Jesus not just as a meditative exercise but also with the expectation that God will work through those promises in our lives.

DISCIPLESHIP COMMUNITY

OPEN WITH PRAYER

Ask for a volunteer to open with prayer. Rotate who does this each time you get together. Praying in front of people may scare you, but it is worth growing in the practice. Praying together is part of what the Body of Christ does. Not only is it our connection to God but it also gives an example of how we live on this discipleship journey.

FROM LAST TIME

How was church? What impacted you? Share with the group how it has helped you in your discipleship journey.

DISCUSSION

1. What jumped out to you in this chapter?

2. Had you heard of Gnosticism before reading this chapter? If you had, where from?

3. Do you ever feel as if there is some secret knowledge just out of your reach that will allow you to fully understand God? How does that feel?

4. What does it mean for you to be both fully spiritual and fully physical?

5. How do you spend personal time in the Bible? What are some helpful practices you have found?

6. Did reading about how God has used physical means to bless His people give you any insight into the Word and Sacraments? What was that insight?

DO IT

Spend personal time in the Word. Share your plan of how you will spend time in Scripture between now and the next time you are all together. Be prepared to share one way that practice has blessed you the next time you're together.

CLOSING

Make sure you know when you are getting together next.

Pray for one another. Take prayer requests and close in prayer. Spread out the prayer requests so as many people are praying as are available.

BEFORE NEXT TIME

Read the "Seek" devotion and chapter 5, and be prepared to share how personal time in Scripture has blessed you.

Seek

Seek the LORD while He may be found; call upon Him
while He is near; let the wicked forsake his way, and
the unrighteous man his thoughts; let him return to the
LORD, that He may have compassion on him, and to our
God, for He will abundantly pardon. For My thoughts
are not your thoughts, neither are your ways My ways,
declares the LORD. For as the heavens are higher than
the earth, so are My ways higher than your ways and My
thoughts than your thoughts.

Isaiah 55:6–9

Trusting the promises of Jesus will lead us, inevitably, to seeking
Him. Throughout the Bible, we see that God does not turn from
those who seek His face. But while seeking God, we often find
more questions than answers. This passage from Isaiah sums it
up nicely. We are to seek the Lord while He is found and near,
but His ways are foreign to us. They are higher and better than
anything we could imagine.

If we cannot fully understand God, does that mean we don't
seek Him? No. There are many things in our life that we do not
fully understand, but that does not stop us from either trusting

they are true or heading over to Google to find out more about them.

Seeking God is not always about knowing things right away. In fact, you may never know fully how God is working. But that does not mean you do not seek Him. Seeking is powered by trusting. When you trust that the promises of Jesus are good and He keeps them, then you seek after Him. You want to learn more.

This section on seeking will get into several different ideas, but the Word of God is the thread that holds them all together. Seeking God is always based in His Word because that is what He has given us to get to know Him.

Stop and take a minute to write down practices that help you engage with Scripture. What works best for you? Do you enjoy group Bible studies or alone time with Scripture? Do you use devotionals as you read to get thoughts on the passages you are reading? Do you enjoy reading different passages related to a specific theme or just reading straight through a book of the Bible? What are some outside resources you go to when your reading sparks a question for which you don't know the answer?

Share your answers to these questions with the group you're reading with. If you came across some questions you don't have an answer to, ask if others in the group do. Learn from them. If you're reading this on your own, consider talking to a friend or your pastor about questions you don't have answers to. This journey is one we take together, helping one another as we go.

Heavenly Father, open my heart to hear Your Word. May seeking You not just be about my own knowledge, but may You use that understanding to deepen my trust in You as I seek. Let the time I spend with You be a blessing to me, and may I learn how Your Word works in my daily life. Amen.

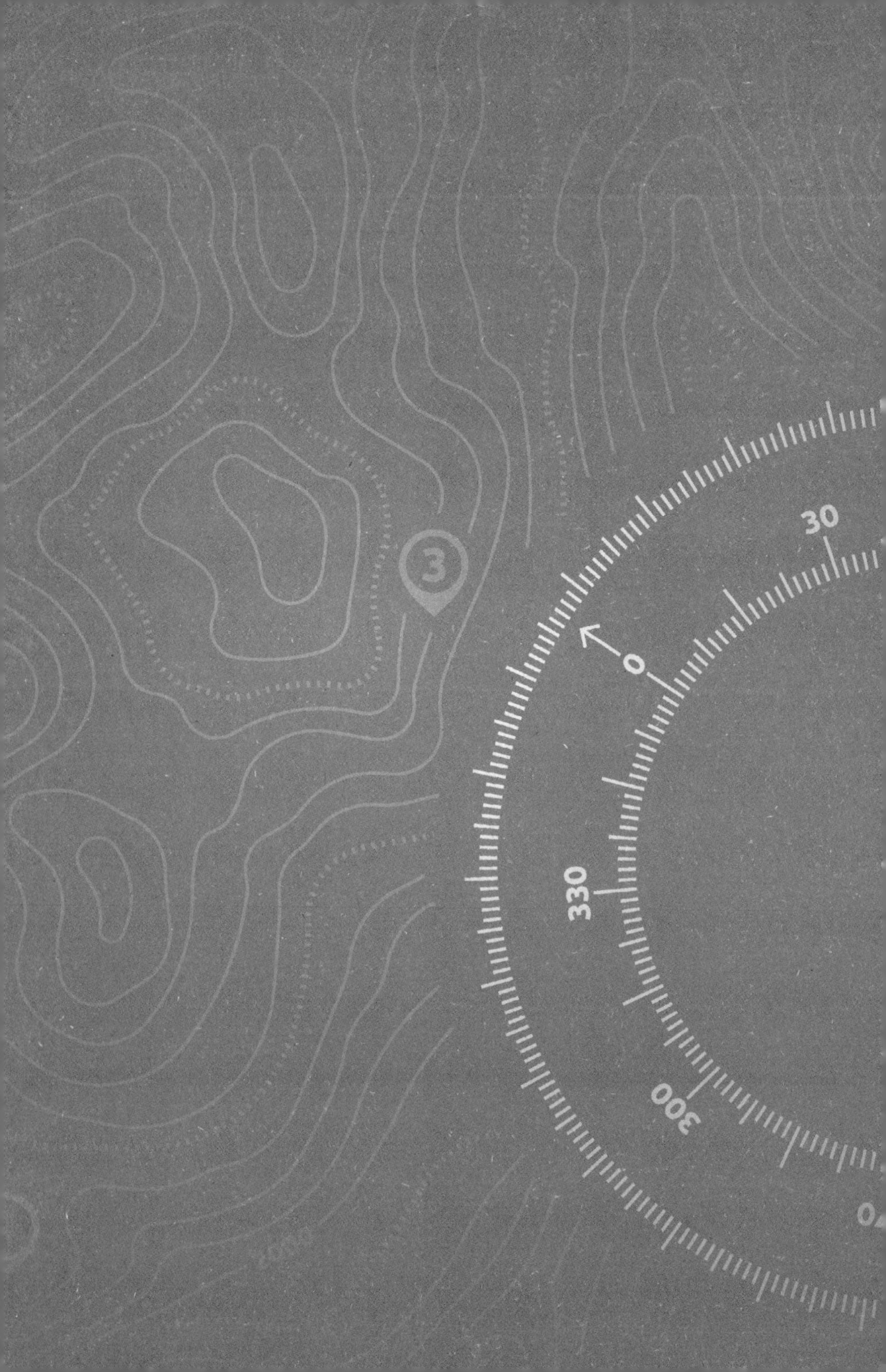
3
30
0
330
300

5

Seeking God

The promises of Jesus provide the source of power for the life of a disciple. With an identity rooted there, the disciple can ask, "Where do I go from here?" Jesus comes to save His people from the effects of sin. The damage that was done because of our disobedience is washed away. Our relationship with Him is made right. But salvation is not simply fire insurance. It is so much more than that.

Saving grace does not allow Christians to stand still in their faith. Salvation always calls people to more. If Jesus could save us, then what more could He do through us? There is purpose behind our salvation. A life of freedom to love Him and love our neighbor lies before us. Commandments are not thrown out the window simply because we break them. Imagine if at our moment of salvation our response was to say, "Great! Now let's get to sinning so we can make this salvation worthwhile!" No. In salvation, we have our eyes opened to see that there is a break between who God created us to be and who we actually are. If His promises are true, then our lives now realign themselves to seek after Him. The promises of Jesus propel us into a life of pursuing Him. This process of re-creation is known as sanctification. It will take a lifetime to grapple with what this looks like on a daily basis.

The traveler on the path of discipleship is fueled by the promises of Jesus. In fact, we have said the Word of God will not only provide fuel but will also be a map along the way. Yet, like all maps, this map does not give the exact picture of what will happen on the journey. Maps set the boundaries and guides for where the journey will lead. But it is on the journey, with one foot in front of the other, that the map truly begins to shine. A traveler appreciates the map not only for its knowledge but also for where it leads. Valleys, mountaintops, open fields, the refreshing springs—the map turns a plan on paper into a journey in the real world.

This is what happens when the disciple seeks after God. His Word is not just a simple book. It is the light of life: "Your word is a lamp to my feet and a light to my path" (Psalm 119:105). The Word of God is more than precepts or commandments; it shows the way we were created to live. However, the study of Scripture cannot be a dissociated event for a disciple. History of what is happening around the verse of Scripture is good. The nuance brought to the Word of God from its original language is good. But if the map becomes the end goal, the way is lost. The disciple must take a simple step farther. The Word of God is meant to be lived, not only read. It must be read in order to be lived, but if it is simply words on a page for the benefit of study and debate, it has lost its meaning. Study, debate, and memorization should buoy the use of the Scriptures, but they are not its end goal, as we are reminded in Scripture itself:

> "Teacher, which is the great commandment in the Law?" And He said to him, "You shall love the Lord your God with all your heart and with all your soul and with all your mind. This is the great and first commandment. And a second is like it: You shall love your neighbor as yourself. On these two commandments depend all the Law and the Prophets." (Matthew 22:36–40)

"All the Law and the Prophets." When Jesus said that, He was speaking of all the known Scriptures at that point in time. All of them hinge on two things: loving God and loving others. Incredibly simple, but incredibly hard. Seeking God is about learning how He is calling you to fulfill those ideas in your life. All of the commands of Scripture are summed up there. The disciple's discernment is simple: should I do a thing? Well, does it love God and love others? If the answer to the second question is yes, then the answer to the first question is yes. The promises of Jesus are not meant to be locked away and hidden only as a secret for the Christian to view in safety and security. No, they are real assurance and adoption into God's family that then propels disciples out into the world to seek how God would have them live in light of these promised realities.

How does this work? Talking about the promises of God is straightforward: These are the promises. You need them in your life. When you wander, return to the promises.

But in seeking God, things start to get messy. The process of seeking God in your life, as a traveler uses a map to follow the trail, is one that does not end. As a wise man once quoted to me, "What does this mean for Monday?" What does it mean in real life? If trusting Jesus leads to seeking Him, then what does seeking look like? It means that we must hear the voice of God working in our lives through His Word and learn to let it guide us forward.

What makes up seeking? Turn back again to head, heart, and hands. Seeking God cannot be only an academic exercise. Too often, seeking is equated with study, but simply studying God does not mean that a person is seeking Him. What about a relationship with God? Is that good enough? Reading Scripture and making everything about oneself is a dangerous path that leads away from discipleship and toward self-help. If not either of those, then seeking God must be about doing the things that Scripture says; only then can one truly be seeking after God. But this, also, is not true. Instead, they must be connected. When seeking is taken as a connection of the head, heart, and hands, then seeking the Lord is about study, application, and experience connected together.

Study

Study of Scripture is an incredible blessing to disciples. In today's world there is quick access to commentaries, study guides, videos, and a whole host of other resources that benefit disciples as they seek Jesus. There is no excuse to be uninformed about the Word of God. Discerning disciples do need to find the resources that are valuable and do not promote rubbish ideas. These valuable tools help us study the Word of God as we seek after Him.

Knowledge of what was happening in and around the times that the Bible was written provides great insight for today. Take the idea of covenant making. God makes covenants with His people throughout Scripture. These covenants find fulfillment in Jesus as the sacrifice for our sins. In the Old Testament, you will often find the translation that God "made a covenant." The Hebrew word "to make" in connection with "covenant" is *karath*, which translates as "to cut off, to cut."[3] In the ancient rites of covenant making, the two parties making the covenant would literally cut an animal in half and pass through the blood, signifying that whoever breaks the covenant would have that blood on them and their family. When God cuts a covenant, the blood should be on His people for disobeying, bowing down to idols, and following the ways of the world. But instead, God places it on His Son! Study of Scripture opens up its depth to us.

Culturally, study can be looked down upon in favor of feelings and experience. Understanding the ins and outs of a subject is often reserved for academics. This method has been applied to the Scriptures as well, where some people leave studying to the theologians. This does not mean these people do not love God or want to seek Him. Rather, they are pushing back against the idea that one must have certain knowledge of Scripture before seeking Jesus. If this were true, only a select few professors, pastors, and armchair theologians could truly be able to seek after God. Instead, disciples hold study in tension. Disciples understand that not everyone is called to the academic pursuit of theology. They value the blessing of those who are and know that they may not have the same amount of knowledge. But disciples also know that trusting only feelings and emotions when it comes to engaging with the Bible is a dangerous pursuit. Do-

---

3   "H3772 - karath - Strong's Hebrew Lexicon (ESV)," Blue Letter Bible, https://www.blueletter
bible.org/lang/lexicon/lexicon.cfm?Strongs=H3772&t=ESV.

ing so leaves one vulnerable to whims, to building on shifting sand rather than the firm foundation. Disciples do not need to know every piece of scholarship concerning the Bible, but they seek to grow in knowledge for the benefit of their journey.

Imagine if a hiker preparing to go on a long through-hike never took time to learn how to read a map. While it may seem like a lost art in the days of digital assistants and GPS, map reading is not an overly hard skill to learn, and you don't have to be a cartographer to do it! Someone spending time out of cell range in the backwoods needs an understanding of how to use a map. The hiker should have the right tools to go along with it, such as a compass and a small ruler, and should learn the key of the map to know how to read the different symbols and glyphs. Time should be taken to research how to identify physical landmarks from their map and how to read elevation lines. A map is an incredible tool for the hiker, and hikers who trust only their feelings or say, "I will learn this as I go," will quickly find it a frustration rather than an aid.

Application

Let's continue with the idea of reading a map. Maps are made to be used. Hanging in my office is a chart of Kodiak Island, Alaska. I spent a summer in college working there. The family I lived with that summer owned the local radar and boat tech store. As I was getting ready to leave, I stopped by and asked if I could buy a chart to take home with me as a souvenir. They gave it as a gift to me. Since then it has hung on dorm room walls, in apartments, and now in my office. It is a cool piece of art that reminds me of an adventurous time in my life—or it did until my brother-in-law came for a visit. The Navy paid for my brother-in-law's undergraduate and graduate degrees. He went through officer candidate school while in college, and after graduation, he served as a submariner. When he was visiting, he walked over to that chart of Kodiak and began to rattle off facts of how he would have used it on his boat. He explained to me the depth charts, the key, and the channels clearly marked. I nodded my head along with his words, dumbfounded by the real-world uses for this chart hanging on my wall. For me it was art; for him it was a tool he could use to bring a submarine to port.

Seeking God must include application of Scripture. Sometimes our faith becomes a wall hanging. Our Bibles are beautiful pieces of art but are never used for their intended purpose. Paul reminds Timothy, "All Scripture is breathed out by God and profitable for teaching, for reproof, for correction, and for training in righteousness, that the man of God may be complete, equipped for every good work" (2 Timothy 3:16–17). The Bible is meant to equip for good works. Seeking after God takes a head-knowledge study of Scripture and connects it to the heart every day through real-world application.

The blessing of studying the Bible is that doing so makes sure our application does not lead us off the path. There will be temptation to force Scripture into what we want to believe. Two key ideas combat that temptation as we apply Scripture in seeking Jesus: Scripture interprets Scripture, and Scripture interprets me.

God does not contradict Himself. When there appear to be contradictions within Scripture, we need discussion and help from people blessed with a deeper understanding of the Bible.

We can't throw out those places or act as if they aren't there. This is why study and asking questions to grow in knowledge is important. But the first place to turn when seeking after God is Scripture itself. When we read the Bible and use the Word of God itself as our first source of interpretation, we learn how God has been working throughout time. His Word does not contradict itself. This interpretation shows how God's Word is true and beneficial in the life of a disciple. Study that pursues application benefits the disciple.

Sometimes we are tempted to make the Bible say what we want it to say. Forcing the Scriptures to defend our side of an argument or the actions that we have taken is a self-focused form of idolatry. Instead, application of Scripture interprets us. It is hard to read the Word of God at times. The Law cuts us deeply. Remember how Jesus talks about murder:

> You have heard that it was said to those of old, "You shall not murder; and whoever murders will be liable to judgment." But I say to you that everyone who is angry with his brother will be liable to judgment; whoever insults his brother will be liable to the council; and whoever says, "You fool!" will be liable to the hell of fire. (Matthew 5:21–22)

Jesus uses the lesson of murder and takes it further. His words are meant to interpret our actions. God looks at what might be explained away as venting or frustration and says, "Nope, that is murder." Our sinfulness does not get an excuse. The Word of God interprets us. It tells us who and how we were created to be. It sets forth the Law of God to let us see our sin, keep us on the path, and show us how to love God and our neighbors. The Gospel is clearly written in its lines to declare our identity as redeemed children of the Kingdom. As we seek after God, His Word applied to our lives changes us because it interprets who we are called to be.

Application of the Word of God takes knowledge and reveals the world around us. Disciples see the world around them through the lens of God's Word and their identity in Christ. No matter what we see, we view it through this Kingdom lens. Learning the difference between prescription and description in the application of Scripture is an incredible benefit. Some things God *prescribes* for His people—the Ten Commandments, the Great Commission, Micah 6:8, and so on and so forth. These can be broken down to the two greatest commandments: love God and love others. There are also *descriptions*, stories and writings that tell who God is, what He is like, and how the world works. It is a good bet that God is not calling for you to march around your neighbor's house once a day for six days and then, on the seventh time on the seventh day, to blow trumpets and watch as their fences and walls come crashing down so you can seize that property as your own, like a modern-day Jericho. Knowledge connected to application helps the disciple to discern what God is saying in His Word.

The Word of God applied to the life of the disciple changes the outlook he or she has of the world. This new lens doesn't let anything slip away. There is no chance or luck. Instead, there is God in the midst of everything. There are lessons in the extraordinary and the mundane. Vocations take on new meaning. Application allows for disciples to see that what they do is connected to the kingdom of God.

Experience

Imagine that you took the time to learn how to read a map. That you put in the time to memorize all the symbols and spent time with a compass learning orienteering. Then, when the big day came to get out on the path, you said, "I know how this works and I bet it would play out nicely, but I think I'll just stay inside." Knowledge of how a map works is good. Understanding how to apply a map in the real world is the next step. But the map must be taken out into the real world and used!

In seeking after Jesus, disciples cannot let their knowledge of Scripture and how it changes their outlook on life be only theoretical. They are meant to live in the ways of Jesus wherever they are. Experience allows disciples to "taste and see that the LORD is good" (Psalm 34:8). It is the natural next step. Seeking after God is also not meant to happen in a bubble. Instead, it is meant to be lived out wherever the disciple goes. Think of all the things experience has taught you over the years. As a child, experience might have taught you that it's not good to touch a hot stove or that ice cream is the best treat for a sore throat. Experiences in school may have taught you about accomplishment and consequences. In adulthood, experience becomes a constant companion in learning how to care for yourself and others. In all these things, you may have the knowledge and the application down, but it is the experiences, some positive and some negative, that reinforce the ideas. The same is true for the journey of discipleship. Experience is a teacher that hammers home the lessons of knowledge and application. Look at when Jesus sends out the seventy-two:

After this the Lord appointed seventy-two others and sent them on ahead of Him, two by two, into every town and place where He Himself was about to go. And He said to them, "The harvest is plentiful, but the laborers are few. Therefore pray earnestly to the Lord of the harvest to send out laborers into His harvest. Go your way; behold, I am sending you out as lambs in the midst of wolves. Carry no moneybag, no knapsack, no sandals, and greet no one on the road. Whatever house you enter, first say, 'Peace be to this house!' And if a son of peace is there, your peace will rest upon him. But if not, it will return to you. And remain in the same house, eating and drinking what they provide, for the laborer deserves his wages. Do not go from house to house. Whenever you enter a town and they receive you, eat what is set before you. Heal the sick in it and say to them, 'The kingdom of God has come near to you.' But whenever you enter a town and they do not receive you, go into its streets and say, 'Even the dust of your town that clings to our feet we wipe off against you. Nevertheless know this, that the kingdom of God has come near.'" (Luke 10:1–11)

Jesus provides the seventy-two with knowledge and application. This group Jesus sends out has been listening to His preaching and teaching. They have been walking alongside Him for some time. Day in and day out over the dusty roads of Israel, they had been listening to and ingesting the teachings of Jesus. Now, He tells them that His teachings are to be taken out. And not only that; there is also a real-world application. There is a harvest in which He is sending them to work. He tells them what they will and won't need. But the important piece is that His teachings are to be taken into the real world. Some will receive them and some will not, but they should trust that the application of God's Word will do what it says. Now look what happens when the seventy-two return:

> The seventy-two returned with joy, saying, "Lord, even the demons are subject to us in Your name!" And He said to them, "I saw Satan fall like lightning from heaven. Behold, I have given you authority to tread on serpents and scorpions, and over all the power of the enemy, and nothing shall hurt you. Nevertheless, do not rejoice in this, that the spirits are subject to you, but rejoice that your names are written in heaven." (Luke 10:17–20)

The seventy-two return after seeing the power of the knowledge of God applied to the real world! They have experienced it. Jesus goes on to tell them that even greater than demons obeying them is the fact that their identities are secure in the Book of Life. Even after the knowledge, application, and experience, Jesus brings them back once again to the promise He has for them, back to the power source.

Knowledge, application, and experience all play into seeking after Jesus. Separately, these all have their potential, but taken together, seeking after Jesus becomes a lifelong pursuit. In most cases, these seekers have gained a deep knowledge of Scripture, look at their lives through a Kingdom lens because of it, and are working daily to see how that knowledge and insight functions in daily life. Disciples seeking after Jesus should not neglect any of these.

When disciples neglect study and knowledge, they will find themselves pulled away by irreverent myth. Without knowledge of the Word of God, any teaching that comes along and makes people feel good will draw them away from the truth of Scripture. There are many doctrines, dogmas, and theologies that sound good but actually pull disciples away from the path. Some of these we have already discussed—those deceptions that would draw people away from the power found in the promises of Jesus. But there are others as well. The old sinful self constantly longs to gain wealth, righteousness, and salvation from within. Study of Scripture combats this. It points back time and again to the promises of Jesus. The identity of the disciple is put in sharp relief to every backward way that might call him or her from the path.

Study and seeking knowledge are for the benefit of the disciple insofar as it does not puff up to pride. Seeking God as a purely academic pursuit that exists only in a theoretical realm will lead to a faith made of fiction. Seeking only the knowledge of God is as useful as reading *The Iliad* or *Beowulf*. It makes the Creator of the universe a myth, one among many. It removes the reality of God from the conversation, making Him instead a topic to be debated and argued about ad nauseum, as if He only existed in the mind of the holder of the knowledge. If application is left to the side, this will happen. Seeking God does not happen only in the realm of thought and theory. It takes place in the everyday lives of disciples. Seeking God happens at kitchen tables, in backyards, on playgrounds, in churches, at coffee shops, and in hospitals. Any place where a disciple treads is a place where seeking God finds purchase and application. Experiencing God is not only spiritual; it is also a real, physical working of God in this world.

But application overemphasized will lead to a moralistic life that seeks gain only for itself. When divorced from study and experience, application creates a faith of magic incantations and formulas: if the right things are done, or the right words are said, then what is desired will be granted. It begets a faith based on works and makes God a vending machine, dispensing whatever we want if we offer the right sacrifice. This God lives far away and does not seek to interact with people unless they follow His rules. There is no love, only a watchmaker who sets His creation to run in the way He made it. It leads to Christians who, in the guise of seeking to be faithful, become self-righteous hypocrites. They wear masks of purity and morality for the world to see. With their mouths, they confess all the right things, but in their hearts festers a hatred of who and what they have become. The power of salvation feels absent because they believe that their works will justify them, that they can pull themselves up by their bootstraps.

Seeking Jesus without experience leads to a dulled picture of the faith. Think about the last time you learned something and then put it into practice. How much deeper does that lesson sit with you now because you have seen it at work? It doesn't always go right the first time or even the seventh time. But each experience shows you more and more how knowledge and application lead to real-world growth.

However, beware of an experience-driven seeking of Jesus. When experience is the only piece used to seek Jesus, it will leave a disciple seeking for the next great high. Everything must be one step up from the last. Then there is no room for ordinary because all that is done must connect with an experience that is even better than the one before it. When that high fades though, all that remains is an emptiness. Then you must search for the next high, all while missing God in the ordinary surrounding you.

Seeking God is about living in tension. Too often tension is equated with conflict, so we humans seek to avoid it. But think of the Golden Gate Bridge. Only because of tension does it carry the load of thousands of vehicles every day. A smooth stone skips across the surface of a lake only because of the surface tension of water. Tension does not need to be a bad thing! Knowledge, application, and experience—none greater than and all as important as the others—are held in tension. A disciple must learn how to keep all of these in play. Sometimes one might drop, but the disciple must come back to all three to seek after God.

The power of the promises of Jesus beckons us disciples to seek after Him. A simple book, the Bible, gives us access to do this. His Word tells us who He is, why He created us, and for what purposes. Through that Word, we are brought back over and over again to the saving grace of Jesus. There we can find knowledge of God—of how, in His wisdom, God created us, saves us, and re-creates us. Through this Word, we understand that our sinful nature was not His intention. A lifetime cannot fully discover the many facets and depths of God. However, seeking a knowledge of who He is will change the lifetime we have.

Seeking God does not remain on the page, however. It is meant to be part of everyday life. The lens of the Kingdom informs our relationships to creature, creation, and Creator. There is no excuse for leaving knowledge to rest and gather dust. Instead, we take knowledge into all the places we go as disciples. Homes should be filled with a discovery of the majesty of God. Places of work are a laboratory to love God and neighbors. Subdivisions, city blocks, parks, restaurants, lakes, schools are all venues for disciples to pursue God among the ordinary and extraordinary.

From the cradle to the grave, we disciples seek after God. There will be days of incredible growth. Other seasons will be simply putting one foot in front of the other. Yet, applying knowledge to our life experiences shows a small glimmer of the Kingdom that is to come. These experiences will solidify seeking after God. They will be the echoes of the new heaven and the new earth. They will be loud, thunderous cracks of God breaking into our life. They will be the whisper of a spring wind. Sometimes, they will simply be our alarm reminding us to start our day in the Bible and in prayer.

Seeking after God will be a pursuit of a lifetime. It will involve tension and heartache, but the joy of salvation will always be present. Fueled by the Gospel, this pursuit will be straightforward but strenuous. There is no excuse not to do it. We don't have to be smart enough, holy enough, or in tune enough. Again, there is only one qualification to be a disciple: be a baptized member of the Kingdom. Do not let anything stop you from starting, or getting up and going again, today. Seeking after God is not done in ivory towers; it is done on the trail. Grab your map and your compass and get out there!

OPEN WITH PRAYER

Ask for a volunteer to open with prayer. Rotate who does this each time you get together. Praying in front of people may scare you, but it is worth growing in the practice. Praying together is part of what the Body of Christ does. Not only is it our connection to God but it also gives an example of how we live on this discipleship journey.

FROM LAST TIME

How did personal devotional time go? How did it bless you?

DISCUSSION

1. What jumped out to you in this chapter?

2. Do you try to apply the ideas of study, application, and experience in your connection to seeking God in His Word? How do you do that?

3. How do you think you can keep study, application, and experience in tension with each other as you seek God?

4. Which of the three (study, application, experience) comes more naturally to you? Why?

DO IT

Look at your personal time in Scripture. You are seeking God. Are you missing any pieces of study, application, or experience? Work this week to add them into your time in the Bible. Be ready to share next week how that went.

CLOSING

Make sure you know when you are getting together next.

Pray for one another. Take prayer requests and close in prayer. Spread out the prayer requests so as many people are praying as are available.

BEFORE NEXT TIME

Read chapter 6 and be prepared to share how adding one of the three central ideas went for your personal study time.

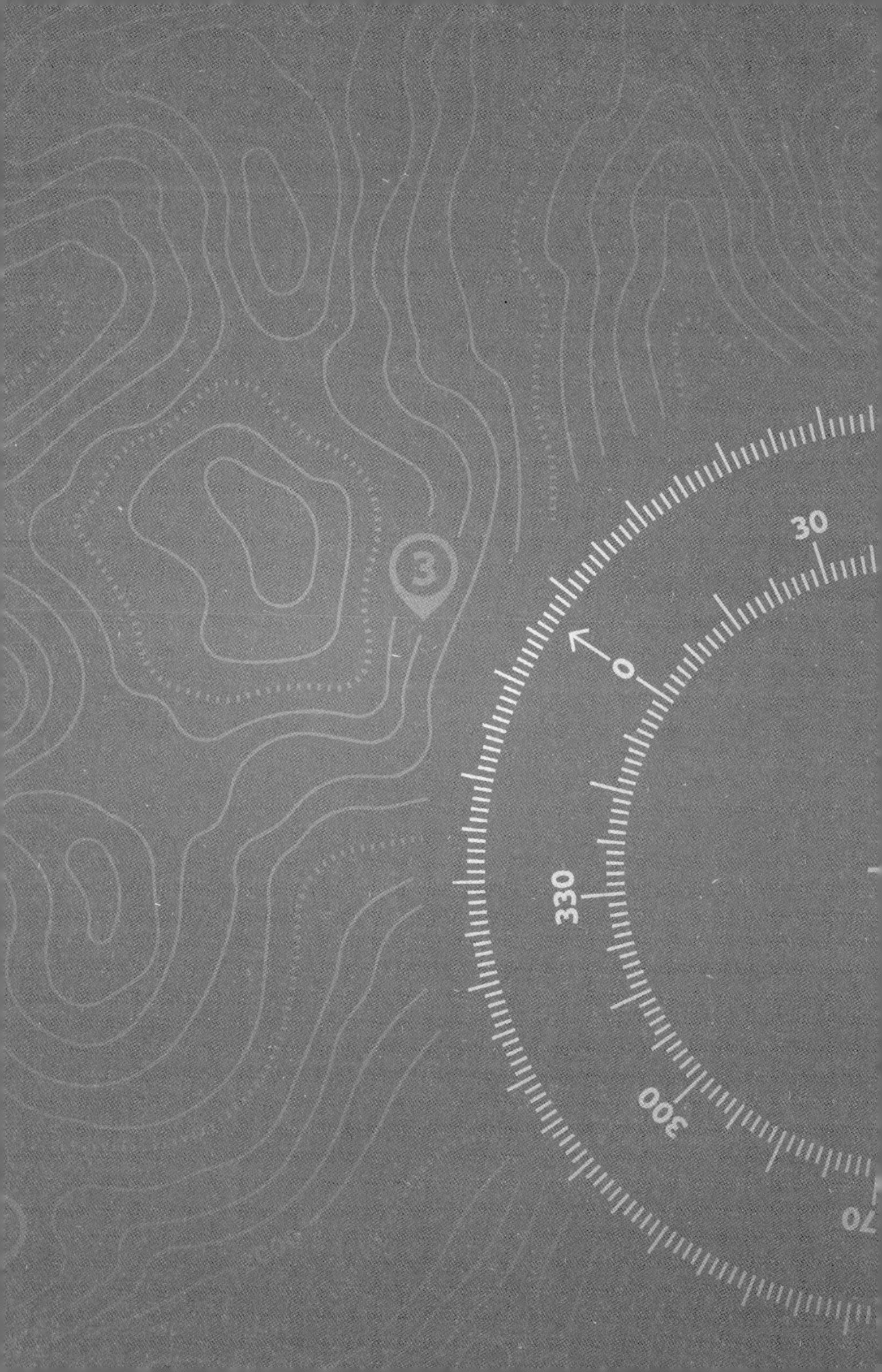
3
30
0
330
300

6

Hearing from God

Hearing from God is a strange idea. There are stories throughout history of people who thought they had heard from God. An audible, angel-from-heaven, do-not-fear, voice-of-the-Almighty moment. Extraordinary circumstances in which people would say that God commanded them to do something. It even happens throughout Scripture. People hear God. Adam and Eve walked in the Garden with God. Abraham was given the promise of his descendants directly from God. Gideon experienced God speaking by dew on a fleece, or not on a fleece . . . honestly, Gideon was a little weird. God called Moses through a burning bush. The prophets delivered messages from God to His people. Mary was visited by an angel. Apostles, followers, and crowds heard God while Jesus walked the paths of Israel. Even the high priest heard God talk when Jesus confessed who He was. Paul heard from Jesus on the road to Damascus. John received visions of the Kingdom that is to come. God speaks to His people.

Yet, when was the last time you heard a booming voice call your name as you sipped your morning coffee? It seems odd that God would function in this way for so long and then change His modus operandi in our present day and age. Did God stop speaking to His people?

The answer is no. God has never stopped speaking to His people. In fact, He has not changed how He does this since the fall of humanity. There are those who are called out. Prophets and apostles, disciples who became the writers of Scripture who heard His voice. These were the people tasked with bringing the ways and will of God to His people. Through the Bible, the voice of God is present in our daily lives.

Too often we make hearing from God overcomplicated. We assume that one must be studied enough to parse the Word of God with a deep knowledge of the original languages and the nuances of Scripture or have a mystically empowered faith that pushes into the supernatural. These seem unattainable. It is as if one must have the right knowledge to truly parse the Word of God, or exist on a different spiritual plane to declare what God is doing (both examples of Gnosticism).

What if hearing from God is much simpler? If the Word of God is truly what we confess it to be, alive and active, then it must work for the everyday disciple. One does not have to be the smartest biblical scholar, but knowledge is important. Achieving a deeper spirituality and gaining unknown insights because of a mystical faith is not the goal, but experience will be a key teacher along the journey. As we disciples live in the tension of knowledge and experience, applying the knowledge through experience, God's Word speaks into our daily lives. This is not simply a type of Bible study nor is it some monk-like trance; instead, it is diving into the Word, expecting that it will speak into your life in a real way.

Guardrails

Before we dive into hearing from God, let's set boundaries to keep us in check. We need to understand several things before beginning this process. In the history of the Church, people have used the idea of hearing from God to gain earthly riches and power. They distort the Word of God and use it for their own self-centered purposes. When learning how to hear from God, disciples must be aware of this fact; the enemy will seek to twist for evil what God has intended for good.

Setting up guardrails keeps us safe and focused. The purpose of barriers in general, and on roads specifically, is to keep travelers safe. They are, most of the time, a constant reminder of where to go and, in the worst-case scenarios, a brutish force used to immediately cease momentum in a direction that could cause greater harm.

SCRIPTURE INTERPRETS SCRIPTURE

This is the message we have heard from Him and proclaim to you, that God is light, and in Him is no darkness at all. If we say we have fellowship with Him while we walk in darkness, we lie and do not practice the truth. But if we walk in the light, as He is in the light, we have fellowship with one another, and the blood of Jesus His Son cleanses us from all sin. If we say we have no sin, we deceive ourselves, and the truth is not in us. If we confess our sins, He is faithful and just to forgive us our sins and to cleanse us from all unrighteousness. If we say we have not sinned, we make Him a liar, and His word is not in us. (1 John 1:5–10)

The first guardrail is one that we discussed in the previous chapter. God will not contradict Himself. There will never be a point when a disciple hears something from the Word of God that then contradicts another part of that Word. Historically, humans have used the Bible to justify everything from unjust wars to slavery. Had this guardrail been in effect for them, there would have been a harsh stop to this evil use of the Word of God.

Selfish desire is always lurking in the sinful self. While a disciple's identity is founded in Jesus' promises, the process of re-creation, or sanctification, takes a lifetime. Until we fall asleep in Christ or He comes again, there will be a constant battle between the ways of Jesus and the ways of sin in our lives. Acknowledging this fact is not weakness. Instead, it proves true these words of Scripture: "But He said to me, 'My grace is sufficient for you, for My power is made perfect in weakness.' Therefore I will boast all the more gladly of my weaknesses, so that the power of Christ may rest upon me" (2 Corinthians 12:9). Confessing this shortfall is not about self-deprecation; rather, we declare the promises of Jesus over our weakness. It is accepting the reality of the world while hoping in Jesus. This does not release disciples from their pursuit of sanctification but instead empowers them through returning, once again, to the power of the promises of Jesus.

Scripture interpreting Scripture allows disciples to discern the voices around them. Are they hearing from God, the evil one, or their own unsanctified flesh? Putting this boundary in place assists disciples as they seek after the voice of God in the midst of the shouting of this fallen world.

THE TWO GREATEST COMMANDMENTS

> And one of them, a lawyer, asked Him a question to test Him. "Teacher, which is the great commandment in the Law?" And He said to him, "You shall love the Lord your God with all your heart and with all your soul and with all your mind. This is the great and first commandment. And a second is like it: You shall love your neighbor as yourself. On these two commandments depend all the Law and the Prophets." (Matthew 22:35–40)

All the Law and the Prophets hang on these two commands: love God and love others. It may seem like these two commandments keep popping up in this book. The reason? They simplify the disciple's journey. There are so many decisions to be made in the lifelong journey of trusting, seeking, and following. Many well-meaning people have tried to build formulas for how to discern the will of God. But in the end, the simplest way to know if a decision is right or wrong comes down to this: Does it love God? Does it love my neighbor?

When seeking the voice of God, these two commandments form one of the strongest barriers. If you are seeking the voice of God and believe that you are supposed to do something that doesn't honor and love God, don't do it! Does it not love your neighbor? Again, avoid it! These simple ideas can be placed into the hard places of life. Understanding how they function in the hardest situations will be a lifelong pursuit. While simple, these two commandments can take on the most strenuous of situations. It will not always be easy, but it will lead back to the voice of God.

LIVING IN THE UNKNOWN

> God said to Moses, "I AM WHO I AM." And He said,
> "Say this to the people of Israel: 'I AM has sent me
> to you.'" (Exodus 3:14)

Sometimes you will not know. God spoke and created the world. He allowed His Son to come to the earth and die for the created. What we know of Him is found in His Word, but even then, He is more than one book. There will be times, even when seeking to hear from God, when He will remain unknown and unknowable. This is not punishment. It is the simple fact that the created cannot fully comprehend the Creator.

This guardrail is set up to protect disciples from heartache. No matter how long one has on the earth, no matter how much time one dedicates and devotes to the pursuit of the journey of faith, God will remain more than can be comprehended. If discipleship were about attaining complete knowledge of God, disciples would constantly be disappointed and dejected. Instead, understanding that God is more than can be imagined, disciples can find contentment in the blessing of what they know of Him. There is joy in limitation. It proves once again that God cares for His people. Limits are not meant to hinder but to allow disciples to seek the ways of God knowing He is good even if they do not fully understand Him. It is a blessing to pursue God in the knowledge that He is greater than anything we had hoped.

COMMUNITY

> Let us hold fast the confession of our hope without
> wavering, for He who promised is faithful. And let

us consider how to stir up one another to love and good works. (Hebrews 10:23–24)

Hearing from God does not happen in a vacuum. Brothers and sisters in Christ are a vital part of the process, another guardrail. Stirring up one another to love and good works means that we, the fellow disciples on the journey, work together. We do not sit alone in a room to decide what God has said. Too often, this leads to ramming through the previously mentioned guardrails and off into the darkness. The Body of Christ is given as a gift to keep us on the path. They call out to us when we are going astray, pulling us back to the promises of Jesus. While hearing God may happen in solitary quiet time or devotions, do not let it remain there. Instead, bring it before close Christian friends. Ask for the wisdom of pastors, elders, Bible study leaders, and those you look up to in the faith. The Body of Christ will not only help keep you on the path, but they will encourage you and call you forward!

The Three Questions

Seeking Jesus is an everyday, ordinary, and supernatural pursuit. Those are three strange words to string together. But when isn't that how God works? His Word, His Sacraments, the Church, His people. Everyday, ordinary, and supernatural. "Everyday" and "ordinary" should not be seen as derogatory. They are a gift. Seeking Jesus does not have to be a mountaintop experience. Many times, it happens at the kitchen table. In seeking to hear Jesus speak into your life, remember that He does so through simple, everyday, ordinary, supernatural experiences.

There are many ways that this could happen. The Church has been doing this in different forms and fashions since it was instituted. It is not about incantations or extemporaneous prayers. Hearing from God is not about finding a hidden revelation or hearing an audible voice. Instead, there is a simple way of letting the Word of God speak into your life. For the process of this discipleship journey, we will use three questions to walk the path of hearing and seeking God.

WHAT IS GOD SAYING?

If God's Word is living and active, then God is speaking to us through it. This is not an impersonal book of morals or fables. The Bible is the power of God delivered to His people. When seeking after Him, the first question the disciple asks is, "What is God saying?"

This question has two aspects: a communal one and a personal one. Communally, the disciple asks this question in terms of how this piece of Scripture fits into the overall narrative of the Bible. It is about understanding the original audience, the time frame of when this piece of Scripture was written, and what it is working to address. Knowledge of the Bible is important in this phase of hearing from God. Studying both His Word and outside sources helps fill in the picture of what is being said. Every piece of His Word is part of a whole and cannot be used as a source text to prove a point. It is taken as a part of the whole, meant for the whole Church. This reminds the disciple that he or she is not alone. Hearing from God is not about individuals wanting to find the oracle to live their best lives. It instead is recognizing that Scripture speaks to all people of God as a larger narrative of His love for His creation.

Communally understanding God's Word leads to a personal knowledge of it. When time is spent in study and community, disciples can see that they are not detached from the story that God is telling. What they recognize is that they are not the main character. This recognition frees them from the responsibility of having to have all the answers or being the savior of others. God's Word can, in freedom, speak directly to them. It is not about some kind of new revelation; instead, it is seeing that God's Word actively applies to everyday life. The discipleship journey seeks God in sanctuaries, dining rooms, bedrooms, cubicles, and playgrounds. What God speaks relates to all aspects of the disciple's life.

Seeking to hear from God means that we can answer the question "What is God saying?" from thirty thousand feet and also from the ground. Give it a try with the parable of the prodigal son. Take a moment to read through it and underline whatever stands out to you:

> There was a man who had two sons. And the younger of them said to his father, "Father, give me the share of property that is coming to me." And he divided his property between them. Not many days later, the younger son gathered all he had and took a journey into a far country, and there he squandered his property in reckless living. And when he had spent everything, a severe famine arose in that country, and he began to be in need. So he went and hired himself out to one of the citizens of that country, who sent him into his fields to feed pigs. And he was longing to be fed with the pods that the pigs ate, and no one gave him anything. But

when he came to himself, he said, "How many of my father's hired servants have more than enough bread, but I perish here with hunger! I will arise and go to my father, and I will say to him, 'Father, I have sinned against heaven and before you. I am no longer worthy to be called your son. Treat me as one of your hired servants.'" And he arose and came to his father. But while he was still a long way off, his father saw him and felt compassion, and ran and embraced him and kissed him. And the son said to him, "Father, I have sinned against heaven and before you. I am no longer worthy to be called your son." But the father said to his servants, "Bring quickly the best robe, and put it on him, and put a ring on his hand, and shoes on his feet. And bring the fattened calf and kill it, and let us eat and celebrate. For this my son was dead, and is alive again; he was lost, and is found." And they began to celebrate. Now his older son was in the field, and as he came and drew near to the house, he heard music and dancing. And he called one of the servants and asked what these things meant. And he said to him, "Your brother has come, and your father has killed the fattened calf, because he has received him back safe and sound." But he was angry and refused to go in. His father came out and entreated him, but he answered his father, "Look, these many years I have served you, and I never disobeyed your command, yet you never gave me a young goat, that I might celebrate with my friends. But when this son of yours came, who has devoured your property with prostitutes, you killed the fattened calf for him!" And he said to him, "Son, you are always with me, and all that is mine is yours. It was fitting to celebrate and be glad, for this your brother was dead, and is alive; he was lost, and is found." (Luke 15:11–32)

From thirty thousand feet, the disciple is able to see what Jesus is teaching. He is showing the love that God has for us. The father gives his sons great gifts, and they squander them. One son runs away and spends all his money on wild living. The other remains at home working hard, yet he ignores the fact that he has the gifts of the father at his fingertips. In both cases, the father comes to the sons. He runs to meet the prodigal at the end of the road when he returns. When the other son waits outside the party, indignant that he has been good and the father has done nothing for him, the father once again comes out, leaving the party to entreat with his son. It is a marvelous story of God's love for us. When seeking God, discerning this is part of the process of hearing Him, of seeing the whole picture.

But it doesn't stop there. The disciple then begins to ask questions of what this parable means on the ground, in his or her life. How is it personally alive? Maybe the disciple has taken some of the blessings of God and spent them on sinful behavior, like the prodigal son. Or, as often is the case for me, the disciple relates to the brother who remained home. "Why does he get the party? I've done all the right things, stayed and done the work of being a good Christian, so why do you throw this sinner a party and I get nothing?!" Here, God calls the disciple to remember that He is close at hand. The gifts of His power and grace have not left, nor has the joy that He finds in calling the disciple His child.

"What is God saying?" seeks to hear the Word of God as a whole and also how it is alive in the life of the disciple.

WHAT IS GOD CALLING ME TO DO?

If God's Word is active daily in the lives of His people, then He is calling them toward action. This is where it might get a little tricky and have a bit of a learning curve. How do we take God's Word and apply it to our daily lives? This is when we especially need guardrails in place, to make sure we stay on the path as we apply how we hear God in our lives. God will not speak against Himself; He will work to do as He has always done. But His Word will directly apply to each person. God is not in the business of simply speaking and then letting His words hang in the air. There is an expectation that they will be put into use.

Go back again to the parable of the prodigal son. If God is declaring His love for His children, that He will come and meet them where they are, what is He calling you to do? It all depends on what is going on in your life. Are you the son who ran away or the son who stayed and is bitter? Maybe you just need the reminder of how deeply God loves you. Or are you missing the fact that God has gifts ready to give you? Are you missing the fact that for both the sons, the father readily gives of what He has? There are many things to connect with in the story, which is underlaid by the powerful promise that God meets His people where they are. For the sake of discussion, let's say you read this parable and connect with the story of the older brother. You feel that indignation; you have been following God, so where are your blessings? Conviction hits as you realize that what God is calling you to is simple: His gifts are already with you; just ask. Latch onto that. God has come out to meet you and is not only reminding you of the gifts He has already given you but also that all you have to do is ask to see how He will bless you more. What is God calling you to do? To recognize His love for you and the gifts He has given to you.

WHAT IS MY NEXT STEP?

What is God saying? This is a question about knowledge. What is God calling me to do? This question applies that knowledge in your life. What is my next step? Here, we take that knowledge and application and put it into practice. Now, this is specifically phrased. The question is not about some long-term plan, your destiny, or a mountaintop experience. It's literally about your next step. On a long journey, sometimes the only thing that can be done is to focus on one more step.

As a disciple, sometimes all you can focus on is one small step. Make a plan, and then take that step. Simple is the best way to go. Why? Because simple is hard to mess up. When we try to make a plan to seek God, we often get in our own way. What started as hearing God speak into our life might quickly turn into a burden that we have taken entirely on our own shoulders instead of seeking and trusting Him. Keeping a plan simple allows you to see what the Holy Spirit will do. Watch as a simple plan becomes a blessing, not because of your works but because of what God has done for you in the midst of it. When you hear God through His Word, apply it to your life, and then take the next step, you will see that He fulfills His promises. It might not always look like you expect—in fact, you'd be surprised how often it doesn't—but God will work. This is not some kind of prosperity move either. There is no formula where if you seek God in a certain way, He will then bless you in the exact way you want. No, this about trusting that when you seek God, He will keep His promises.

Let's give this question a shot. How might we answer it when looking at the story of the prodigal son? In that passage, God is speaking of the love for His children. In this situation, it is a calling to remember that you are loved, that God has blessed you with His gifts. A simple next step might go like this: three times in the coming week, take five minutes to write down things you are grateful for in your life, taking time to pray and say thank You for them. It is simple and takes fifteen minutes throughout the span of a week. Maybe at the end of the week, take a moment to write down how this has changed your outlook.

In these three questions, you will not find the secrets of the universe. They were not discovered in a secret chamber below a monastery. There is nothing special about them. All they do is focus on how to hear God from His Word. Here, the process is to take knowledge, see the application it holds in life, and then go and experience how it is lived in the world. When seeking God, humans try to find either a formula for blessing or an express elevator to spiritual mountaintops. But these three questions remain ordinary, not special. They are just a way to check in and pay attention while connecting with the Word of God. They can be used during personal devotion, after group Bible study, or even to process Sunday's sermon.

You will not find salvation in these questions. Instead, they will point back to the promises of Jesus. As we hear from God through His Word, these questions help disciples to step outside themselves, to view the text as changing them, not the other way around. Walking through these questions correctly, or incorrectly, will not have an impact on the grace given by Jesus. They are to help us discover how our central identity changes how we interact with the world. Always, the foundation of a Christian's identity is the saving work of Jesus. How this reality interacts in your home, work, neighborhood, and church is what these three questions are built to affect.

Starting a process of answering these questions and hearing from God will not be a short endeavor. In fact, this will probably be a practice you will use for the rest of your life. Learning the ins and outs, getting it right and wrong, working past the awkward feeling of the woodenness of the questions are all a part of growth in seeking God. At some point, the questions may not even come to mind; you might just start interacting with Scriptures in the ways the questions are designed to encourage. Again, these questions are not holy or sacred. Instead, they are training wheels put in place to help steady and direct until balance and direction become second nature. Hearing from God is not about some great spiritual revelation. Instead, we seek after knowledge of His Word, learn how it applies to life, and then do what God has called us to do.

Just Do It

Seeking after God can happen only if you do it. It is easy to talk about the complex study habits, devotionals, and resources you might use. Instead of building all kinds of complex systems, seeking and hearing God is simple: you have to just do it. Sit down with a Bible, resources, prayers, and the like, and dive into it. We will be tempted to try to find the exact right way to do it. Instead, just start. Every Christian has unique ways in which to connect while seeking God. Instead of trying to decide what works best for you first, just start and see what sticks. Ask others what works for them. Take and mold those things to your own practice. Another important aspect is to have resources that help you dig deeper—books, websites, or people—because, guaranteed, there will be a point when you come across something in Scripture you don't understand. Let it be a speed bump and not a ditch. Have in place systems that can help you find an answer. Get in touch with a pastor or Bible study leader. That person will be more than willing to give you an answer or find one with you. Ask good questions and struggle through hard concepts and ideas. Do not let your faith remain in the liquid food stage; chew some steak. But start seeking God.

Learn to see God speaking in your everyday life. Be so deeply entrenched in the Bible that as you go about your day, you can see how God is working in the ways He promises He will. My dad, who is a pastor and one of my chief mentors in the faith, explained it to me when I was growing up like this: Imagine you decided one day to become a bird watcher. You get a book on birds and a pair of binoculars, and you hop online to find the best bird-watching spots in your area. Then you go out to start bird watching. You spend an hour and spot half a dozen crows and a wren or two, but nothing crazy. But you are committed, so you regularly keep going out. You keep spotting the normal things but also begin to know where to look for the rarer birds. The places where you might spot cardinals, blue jays, or the elusive golden-cheeked warbler start popping out to you. Because of the time you spend specifically bird watching, you begin paying attention to the birds around you as you walk into work and run errands—you start to see them wherever you go.

This is what seeking God will do in your life. As you ask the questions and remain in His Word, you will begin to see how that Word is at work all around you. The more time you put into seeking, the greater the reward will be in finding. God is working. His Word speaks into our lives, telling us how He works. Learn about that Word. See how it works in your life. Live it out and watch how it sanctifies you as go.

Practice It Together

If you are reading this book in a discipleship community, take some time around these questions. In fact, maybe take a pause moving forward and spend time learning what these questions feel like in real life. It will be important to support one another as you grow in answering these questions. Remember, it is not some overly holy idea. It is just simple questions that get you hearing God, seeing His work in your life, and then taking one more step. Often, you will find that in taking that step, God will teach you more. The Holy Spirit will take that small thing and work to build it into what you need to learn and the ways you need to grow. Sometimes those steps will actually lead you to the realization that you need to rest and slow down. Other times they may call you to more than you could have imagined.

Time in discipleship community in the chapters going forward will incorporate these questions, but you might need a little more experience than that. Remember the bird-watching analogy? Do not be discouraged if this feels strange or awkward. Grow into it. Spend time learning how to see God working in your everyday life. If your group wants more practice in the three questions before moving forward, that is great! Slow down and do it. Here is a process to work through the three questions together over a couple of weeks.

WEEK 1

1. Pick some Scripture to read together. I recommend something from the Book of John.

2. Have one person take notes for your group, writing down each person's answer to the questions.

3. Walk through the questions together.

4. Using the notes, commit together to check in with one another to testify how God is at work through His Word and the next steps.

5. Send texts, emails, or carrier pigeons to ask how people are doing with their next steps.

WEEK 2

1. Start with prayer.

2. Share stories of next steps. If some didn't do their next steps out of busy-ness or fear, encourage them.

3. Celebrate what God is doing!

4. Assign Scripture reading for the next time together. Keep connecting throughout your time apart about how God is working.

Rinse and repeat!

You don't have to speed through these ideas. They take time. Take the time your group needs to encounter them. This book isn't a race to be finished. Think of it more like a leg of a journey that will take your lifetime.

OPEN WITH PRAYER

Ask for a volunteer to open with prayer. Rotate who does this each time you get together. Praying in front of people may scare you, but it is worth growing in the practice. Praying together is part of what the Body of Christ does. Not only is it our connection to God but it also gives an example of how we live on this discipleship journey.

FROM LAST TIME

How did changing up your personal time in Scripture go?

DISCUSSION

1. What comes to mind when you hear someone say he or she is hearing from God?

2. What do you think about the process of hearing from God that is presented in this chapter?

3. How does each guardrail help protect you from getting lost?

THE THREE QUESTIONS

This will now be a section each week for your group to work through. The three questions are a key part as you hear from God's Word and seek to act on it. Make this a regular activity even after you finish the book. This simple process can be done with any piece of Scripture. For this week, use the parable of the prodigal son found in Luke 15:11–32 (also listed earlier in this chapter). Answer the three questions. Be prepared to share next week!

1. What is God saying?

2. What is God calling me to do?

3. What is my next step?

CLOSING

Make sure you know when you are getting together next.

Pray for one another. Take prayer requests and close in prayer. Spread out the prayer requests so as many people are praying as are available.

BEFORE NEXT TIME

Read chapter 7, answer the questions for that chapter, and be prepared to share your answers to the three question with the group!

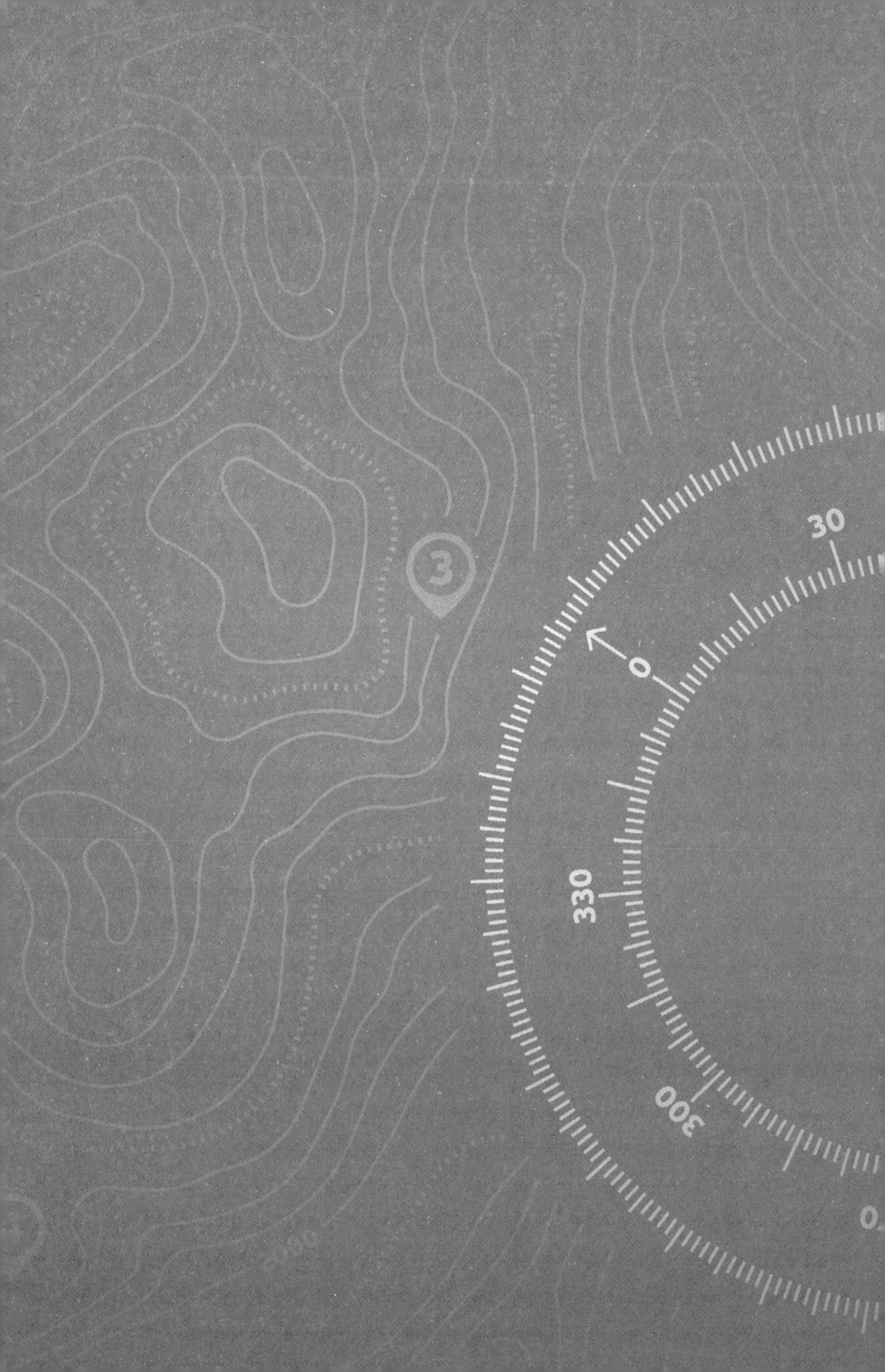
3
30
0
330
300

Community

In the beginning, God creates. It is incredible. Seas, mountains, skies, animals—He makes all of it. Then as He comes to the end, He looks around and wants to create something like Him, His image bearer in this new universe. From dirt and breath, He creates Adam. Then God makes a simple statement: "It is not good for man to be alone." God then takes a rib and creates woman so that man may have a companion in this new creation. It is not good to be alone.

As Jesus teaches and models for His disciples the ways of the Kingdom, He ends up sending them out to announce that Kingdom. But He does not send them alone. No, two by two they are sent. Companions on the road, carrying the message of the Kingdom into the countryside. Jesus tells them to take nothing, but He does make sure they have a partner. In this new, pivotal task, they are not alone.

When the Church begins to spread like wildfire after Jesus' ascension, it did not do so as a singular pursuit. The Book of Acts speaks of the many houses that became places of gathering. Christians began pooling together their belongings and sharing with those who were in need. It was the community of Christ coming together. Missionary journeys were taken with brothers and sisters in the faith. The Church always gathers and is sent in community.

All of this is a reflection of God Himself. Gathered in the divine Trinity of Father, Son, and Holy Spirit, God exists in a beautiful, mysterious community.

We often believe an old lie: you can do this better on your own. There is a strange stigma that would pressure us to consider any help a hindrance or weakness instead of a blessing. This is not true, and especially so on the discipleship journey. The path is full of those who have gone before and those who will come behind. Some will even be in the same phase of the journey. Once again, God takes and uses His creation to bless His people. Seeking God will have solitary moments, but it is not a lonely pursuit.

Historically, there have been movements to isolate from others to find God. Life lived in community can be messy—just read the New Testament letters! Paul is constantly reminding these new churches not only of the promises of Jesus but also of how to get along with one another. However, the response should not be to retreat from the community and seek God in isolation. This often leads to a mystical outlook of God that divorces the spiritual life from the normal rhythms of the world. It is important to spend time seeking God privately and in personal devotion. Taking time to retreat into creation to engage with Scripture can be a deeply insightful experience. But leaving the Church behind to do so is problematic. As created beings, humans are made to interact with one another. In the community of the Church, we have a supernatural bond of defense, encouragement, and power that can come only from God.

Prone to Wander

Part of the problem in seeking after God is that we trust ourselves too much. That doesn't mean that we shouldn't have self-confidence and determination to move forward. But we also need to remember that we are not God.

There will always be opportunities to wander off the path. Sometimes this happens simply because we have stopped paying attention. Have you ever had a moment when you took one extra step, believing there to be one more stair in a staircase? Or maybe you were walking, messing around on your cell phone, and then tripped over a curb. Maybe you were driving and simply took one wrong turn that led you into a maze of streets that kept you from reaching your destination. When trusting, seeking, and following Jesus, there will be times that you look around and realize, somehow, you have wandered off and become lost.

It happens to all of us—wandering away from the path and toward the alluring temptations in the distance. The Body of Christ exists to call us back. It is a give-and-take. Sometimes we are the ones calling; sometimes we are the ones being called. But God provides for His people with His people. Whether we are chasing after idols, becoming weary, or turning inward on ourselves, the Body of Christ stands ready to be the hands and feet of Jesus along the way.

The previous chapter mentioned community as a guardrail when hearing from God. This is an important function of the Body of Christ. As the Holy Spirit moves to convict followers of Jesus in their daily lives, fellow Christians are often a means through which He acts. There will always be temptation to turn inward, even while seeking God. Our sinful nature would turn seeking God to our own ends, making God into our own tool for judgment and self-righteousness instead of recognizing Him as King. This sinful belief would lead us deeper inward to a place where our own views are correct above all else. The community of faith comes along to knock down these false beliefs and call us back to the ways and promises of Jesus.

This happens throughout Scripture. In the Old Testament, God sent the prophets to point out the ways in which Israel had chased its own desires instead of following Him. John the Baptist was sent to the prepare the way of the Savior and was murdered because he called out the sin of a king. The apostles planted churches throughout the Roman Empire, all the while writing letters to admonish believers to return to grace and live as people of God. It is always within the follower of God to return to sin; the gift of community calls the saint to repentance.

Admonishment from the Body of Christ is a blessing to the disciple. It will never be easy. When sin has taken control or covered a disciple's eyes, the sting of conviction feels painful. But it is the pain of setting a broken bone. It must hurt to heal. When our sin is laid before us, it should cause pain. Our failure and insecurities are laid bare. David was confronted by Nathan. Jesus called Peter Satan. Paul called out Peter over how he treated the Gentiles. This is such an important aspect of faith that Jesus spoke to it in Matthew 18:14–17:

> So it is not the will of My Father who is in heaven
> that one of these little ones should perish. If your
> brother sins against you, go and tell him his fault,
> between you and him alone. If he listens to you,

you have gained your brother. But if he does not listen, take one or two others along with you, that every charge may be established by the evidence of two or three witnesses. If he refuses to listen to them, tell it to the church. And if he refuses to listen even to the church, let him be to you as a Gentile and a tax collector.

Matthew 18 lays out the interactions of the community when it comes to sin. First one-on-one, then a few people, then the church, then treat as a tax collector or Gentile. Even if the unrepentant do not see their sin, they are to be treated with dignity. These verses come between stories of lost things being found. "Treat them as a tax collector or Gentile" is not code for "Shun the unbeliever!" Instead, it is a reminder that the purpose of calling out sinners is to bring them back to the Gospel. Treating fellow believers in this way is to say that they have gone so far as to not be able to hear the whole church. Either they are stubborn in their own ways or have had their heart hardened to this problem of sin in their lives. The goal is not to shame them into brokenness but to bring them back to the promises of Jesus. They have wandered far away; the Church is called to bring them Jesus.

This is a beautiful gift as one seeks after God. Sin may tempt and at times hold sway in life. The community of faith is a gift of people who do not seek their own glory by trampling upon others. Instead, at its core, the Body of Christ is a group of people who see that all fall short of the glory of God. They see that the only hope is Jesus, and when someone starts wandering, they work to bring the person back in loving kindness to the path. This does not always work itself out in this way. All too often, judgmentalism and pride seep into a group of believers. This leads to protection of the group above all else. This breaks churches, communities, and individuals. If the community is to function as it was intended, there must be continual repentance. Satan will work to destroy any good gift and make it a backbreaking burden instead. The Church must be constantly vigilant, always calling itself as a community to greater standards of grace, compassion, kindness, and gentleness as it seeks after God. As part of that community, that is also your function as a disciple. Not only will the community call you back to the promises of Jesus, but as part of a whole, you will also be blessed to be a voice speaking to this truth.

Encouragement

> Therefore, since we are surrounded by so great a cloud of witnesses, let us also lay aside every weight, and sin which clings so closely, and let us run with endurance the race that is set before us, looking to Jesus, the founder and perfecter of our faith, who for the joy that was set before Him endured the cross, despising the shame, and is seated at the right hand of the throne of God. (Hebrews 12:1–2)

It was tax season a few years ago. There had been a few unexpected car-based expenses, and I had missed a couple of things on a form or two. I had just gotten the email from our tax office telling us what we would owe that year. As I read more zeros than I care to admit, my heart dropped. In terms of failures in my life, this was in the top three. I walked into our bedroom and dropped onto the floor next to where my wife was sitting on the bed. Working the words out of my mouth, I confessed to her the errors I had made and how much it had cost. Her eyes were wide. All I could see in them was my failure. There was nowhere else to lay blame except on my shoulders. It was one of my duties to keep track of these things. Laziness had gotten in the way of me getting the job done. Now I had to sit in front of my wife, whom I had vowed to take care of the best I could, and admit utter defeat. You know what that woman of God did? Through her own fear and frustration, she looked at me with compassion, got down on the floor with me, and told me it would be all right. Over and over, when all I could see was my failure, she told me she still loved me. She pulled me back to grace and forgiveness, pointing me to my identity as a child of God. Sitting there on the floor of the bedroom, she proclaimed the promises of Jesus over me. It is one of the most beautiful moments in our marriage.

Later in the week, I called and talked with a friend. He is older than me and had more experience in the world. I shared with him my failings. I brought to him how I felt and how I could feel the failure defining me. He chuckled a little, then shared similar things that had happened with him and his family for similar reasons. In that moment, he shared with me his own struggles and the issues they had caused. He revealed to me some of his own failures. It opened my eyes: I wasn't alone. Here was a man I looked up to as a brother in Christ, someone I always sought to emulate, and he had struggled with similar things I did. He, too, brought me back to the promises of Jesus, telling me that my failure doesn't define me—Jesus does.

Community surrounding me brought me back to my identity. They encouraged me not just with words but with Jesus. It didn't mean that I wouldn't have to learn and grow or that I avoided having to pay off this tax bill, but I learned how to find God in the midst of it. My failure did not separate me from His love.

Weariness can overwhelm the discipleship journey. Our own fears and failures will weigh us down even as we seek after God. The ways of this world will pull at us, hoping to mire us in the mud so that we stop and get lost in self-pity. Here, the Body of Christ comes along and picks us up. They walk into the mud with us, step down, and pull us up. Sometimes they will take our burdens and help us carry them for a while. Other times they throw those burdens away, reassuring us that they were in fact things we need not carry. Jesus proclaims that His yoke is easy and His burden is light (Matthew 11:30). He sends His people to remind us of that fact. It doesn't mean the failure and weariness disappear. Instead, they take on a different meaning in light of the promises of Jesus. The Body of Christ reminds us of that reality. When the road feels weary, when we have messed up again, the family of faith gets down on the ground with us to tell us again of God's steadfast love.

You are not alone. What beauty is found in the words from Hebrews that we are surrounded by a cloud of witnesses! Seeking after God does not happen in a vacuum. Instead, you are surrounded by those behind and ahead. They are there to admonish and encourage you. God provides His people with His people, a group like no other on this earth; a family bound by the blood of Christ. The path of discipleship is not a lonely one. There will be difficult days. Days of forward movement and days when you might feel like you are rolling down the hill. Sometimes it will appear that you are lost in the woods, the path having disappeared below your feet. But there is a blessed gathering. A group of people who will walk alongside you and bring you back. God's people endowed with the Holy Spirit, calling to conviction and encouragement. Listen to them. Learn how to discern what God is teaching you through them. See how His Word connects through life with them.

Sometimes it will be hard to see your progress. A life lived seeking after Jesus and in continual sanctification might at times feel like running in place. So many distractions and temptations reach out to trip up disciples that it might feel like you are constantly looking down to see where the next snare will be. This can become exhausting. When a fellow believer sits down to encourage you and points out the progress you have made, it is invigorating. To slow down and look back, to see that God has fulfilled His promises—what an incredible blessing.

Here is another benefit God gives to those living in community: they are not only blessed but also get to be a blessing. Living in community means that you are also called to help those who have wandered astray. It will be part of discipleship to learn how to exercise Matthew 18 in your own life when you are sinned against and when you see friends and family turning inward and away from God. You are called to love them and call them back to following Jesus. It is not just about you; it is about being a part of the community that supports you. There will be people along the way who mentor and encourage you. They will walk alongside you and admonish you in the ways of the faith, drawing you back to the promises of Jesus. This is also your calling. It does not matter what you do with your life, whether you are a baker, a pastor, an electrician, a teacher, a stay-at-home mom, or a professional athlete. If you are a baptized believer in the saving work of Jesus, you are part of the community of faith, the Body of Christ. The Great Commission applies to you. "Go therefore and make disciples of all nations, baptizing them in the name of the Father and of the Son and of the Holy Spirit, teaching them to observe all that I have commanded you. And behold, I am with you always, to the end of the age" (Matthew 28:19–20). Baptism leads to a life of teaching and observing the ways of God (trusting, seeking, and following). You are a part of that!

A Member of the Body

I appeal to you therefore, brothers, by the mercies of God, to present your bodies as a living sacrifice, holy and acceptable to God, which is your spiritual worship. Do not be conformed to this world, but be transformed by the renewal of your mind, that by testing you may discern what is the will of God, what is good and acceptable and perfect. For by the grace given to me I say to everyone among you not to think of himself more highly than he ought to think, but to think with sober judgment, each according to the measure of faith that God has assigned. For as in one body we have many members, and the members do not all have the same function, so we, though many, are one body in Christ, and individually members one of another. Having gifts that differ according to the grace given to us, let us use them: if prophecy, in proportion to our faith; if service, in our serving; the one who teaches, in his teaching; the one who exhorts, in his exhortation; the one who contributes, in generosity; the one who leads, with zeal; the one who does acts of mercy, with cheerfulness. Let love be genuine. Abhor what is evil; hold fast to what is good. Love one another with brotherly affection. Outdo one another in showing honor. Do not be slothful in zeal, be fervent in spirit, serve the Lord. Rejoice in hope, be patient in tribulation, be constant in prayer. Contribute to the needs of the saints and seek to show hospitality. Bless those who persecute you; bless and do not curse them. Rejoice with those who rejoice, weep with those who weep. Live in harmony with one another. Do not be haughty, but associate with the lowly. Never be wise in your own sight. Repay no one evil for evil, but give thought to do what is honorable in the sight of all. If possible, so far as it depends on you, live peaceably with all. Beloved, never avenge yourselves, but leave it to the wrath of God, for it is written, "Vengeance is Mine, I will repay, says the Lord." To the contrary, "if your enemy is hungry, feed him; if he is thirsty, give him something to drink; for by so doing you will heap burning coals on his head." Do not be overcome by evil, but overcome evil with good. (Romans 12)

Romans 12 is only twenty-one verses, but it will take a lifetime to unpack. It gives a good outline of what it means to be a member of the Body of Christ. The leading verses give a call back to the previous chapter, learning to hear God and discern His voice from His Word. We are called to constantly seek after God to find discernment and renewal. Paul then continues into a description of how one lives in the Body of Christ.

First, we will have gifts that differ from one another's. Not every person needs to be good at everything. The Body of Christ is a reflection of all of creation, uniquely built to function together. Strength and weakness go hand in hand. When it comes to gifts mentioned in the Bible, some people might snicker at the gift of administration. You never find me as one of those people. Why? Just go look at my filing cabinet. Administration is not a gift for me, and I am always in awe of those who do it well. What an incredible gift that the Lord would work in His Body to have strength and weakness come together so that the whole Body can function! Paul calls the Body to celebrate its differences because doing so proves the promises of God once again.

Discovering how you are gifted is not an act of arrogance. Instead, it is acknowledging that God has created people uniquely to do unique things. This is not a destiny theology that sets aside gifting as a desired blessing that will come along to carry you into some supernatural design. It is a blessing from God in how you were created. It means that you don't have to do everything. You get to walk alongside others who are gifted in areas you are not, and vice versa. When members of the Body of Christ discover their strengths and weaknesses, the whole

Body is blessed as God's promises at work in and amongst us are made known.

As a disciple seeking Jesus, learning your giftedness is important. Look at how Paul describes it above: "Having gifts that differ according to the grace given to us, let us use them: if prophecy, in proportion to our faith; if service, in our serving; the one who teaches, in his teaching; the one who exhorts, in his exhortation; the one who contributes, in generosity; the one who leads, with zeal; the one who does acts of mercy, with cheerfulness" (vv. 6–8). The use of gifts is built into the grace given to us, designed through the Holy Spirit at work. It blesses those around us. As we use our gifts, we find out how they work and function in our lives and the lives of others.

These gifts are set up so that none of us would fall into our own pride. In the world, gifts and talents are used to shame others. There is temptation to look down on others who may not have our same capabilities. But not so for the disciples of Jesus. We are to recognize the work of God in us and live in humility, serving one another with the gifts we have been given.

"Outdo one another in showing honor" (v. 10). The verses surrounding this phrase are both encouraging and convicting. What an incredible picture of the community gathered around their baptismal identity, fervent in love and holding fast to what is good. In all of this, they don't seek to elevate themselves or see themselves as more than they are. Instead, they seek honor more for their brothers and sisters than themselves. In community, we function not to bring glory to ourselves but to see the glory of God and to honor those around us. What a backward-seeming idea. But that is what it means to live in this Body. We are called to let go of our vanity and needs, to associate with those the world views as lower than us, because the truth of the matter is that we are all heirs to the kingdom of God.

Finally, Paul points us outward. He admonishes us, "Beloved, never avenge yourselves, but leave it to the wrath of God, for it is written, 'Vengeance is Mine, I will repay, says the Lord.' To the contrary, 'if your enemy is hungry, feed him; if he is thirsty, give him something to drink; for by so doing you will heap burning coals on his head.' Do not be overcome by evil, but overcome evil with good" (vv. 19–21). Love your enemies. That objective seems more attainable while surrounded by the Body of Christ. Maybe someone in the Body might even feel like your enemy—and now we're back to Matthew 18.

What does it look like for you to love your enemies? Every follower of Jesus will have to answer this question. It is commanded by the Savior: "But I say to you who hear, Love your enemies, do good to those who hate you, bless those who curse you, pray for those who abuse you" (Luke 6:27–28). The Body of Christ lives up to these values. Love goes beyond just the people you like. You love those who would persecute you. This is not an easy task. It requires taking a long, hard look at people we dislike and despise, digging deep into the promises of Jesus, and loving those people. It is not by mistake that Paul discusses this along with the way we are to treat and live with the Body of Christ. It is easy to have the head knowledge that we should love our enemies. Also, it probably wouldn't take you long to find people you might want to put in that category. Putting love into real-world action, though, is difficult. Simple, but difficult. Share that burden with your community, with Christian people you trust. Ask them to pray with you for the people you consider your enemies. Live within that blessing.

Discipleship in Community

Everything that has been discussed in this book so far is best used in the midst of community. Discipleship will have solitary moments but should not be undertaken alone. There will be times when you will need to be convicted and called out for sin in your life. There will be times when you will need that from others. So, how do you know when to do that? How does that look in real life? Law and Gospel can give us a quick insight into how this can be applied.

Law and Gospel is a simple theological idea with profound implications. When referring to the Law, you are looking at the ways of God: the commands, edicts, and created systems. Law will be a mirror, curb, and guide. As a mirror, it will show you your sin. Think of the Ten Commandments. Hold that up to your life. Where have you broken one of those commandments this week? Think you're good on the murdering one? Well, Jesus would say that if you've thought ill of someone, then you have murdered them in your heart: "You have heard that it was said to those of old, 'You shall not murder; and whoever murders will be liable to judgment.' But I say to you that everyone who is angry with his brother will be liable to judgment; whoever insults his brother will be liable to the council; and whoever says, 'You fool!' will be liable to the hell of fire" (Matthew 5:21–22). The mirror of the Law shows you that you are sinful.

As a curb, the Law trips you up when you leave the path. What is the point of a curb? To keep you within the boundaries of a roadway. If you are starting to drift, the curb will warn you that you are going the wrong way. It will violently warn you if you just decide to ignore it and go Dukes of Hazzard in your own direction. So, too, the Law. When you decide to blatantly disregard God's ways, it will make you feel it.

Finally, the Law is a guide. It shows you the path. Those commands, edicts, and created systems are built for your prosperity. Look at Adam and Eve in the Garden before the fall. They acted in the way of God because it is good! The Law shows us the way that God created us to be and gives us a guide for how we are to trust, seek, and follow Him.

However, we aren't left with the Law. When the Law holds up a mirror to our sin, it is not to destroy us but rather to show us our need for a Savior. When we run over the curb at full speed, the Gospel reminds us that we can return to the path in repentance. In failure and striving, as we try to live up to the Law as our guide to the way God has called us to live, the Gospel is the balm of forgiveness. The Gospel is the ultimate promise of Jesus, our justification. He is the Savior we need. He brings us back to the path—that which was lost is found. He gently brings us back to following Him, time and again, try after try. In Jesus, we find the power to do the good works laid before us.

The idea of Law and Gospel helps us understand how to interact with others on our discipleship journey in a kind and loving way. When we encounter difficult situations in the Body of Christ, applying Law and Gospel will guide us as we walk together on the path of discipleship. Look for the signs of whether to apply Law or Gospel, conviction or encouragement. Is someone acting in sin or turning inward? If you bring these issues to the person but he or she responds with indignation, then the Law is needed to show the person how he or she is wandering. But if the person is contrite and sees his or her errors, then the Gospel is needed to build up the person and restore him or her in the promises of Jesus. The goal is always to help one another grow in trusting, seeking, and following Jesus. Remember that as you walk the discipleship journey with those around you. Also remember that your own heart and mind will betray you. Let the Law do its work in you, and drink deeply of the springs of the Gospel. It will take time to learn how to apply these principles, but they will be beneficial as you walk together in community.

Do not go alone. Rejoice in the gift of the Body of Christ. Following Jesus is not a solitary act but instead a joy-filled lifestyle spent in community together. Learn to share the three questions with a group of people whom you plan to grow alongside. Worship alongside the great cloud of witnesses. Celebrate together! Invite those who don't yet know Jesus to join. Live in humility, allowing yourself to be convicted by the Body that continually looks out for you. Call others to live in such a way. "Outdo one another in showing honor."

OPEN WITH PRAYER

Ask for a volunteer to open with prayer. Rotate who does this each time you get together. Praying in front of people may scare you, but it is worth growing in the practice. Praying together is part of what the Body of Christ does. Not only is it our connection to God but it also gives an example of how we live on this discipleship journey.

FROM LAST TIME

What are your answers for the three questions? Ask one another, "How can we support you in your next step?" (Helpful hint: Set up a group text to check in and see how everyone's next steps are going!)

DISCUSSION

1. What jumped out to you in this chapter?

2. How has the community helped you as a disciple in your journey thus far?

3. Take a moment to write down the names of the people with whom you are reading this book. Write down one piece of encouragement for each of them. Share together.

4. When was the last time you had to call someone out in their walk of faith? When was the last time you were called out and needed it?

DO IT

Plan something fun to do together as a group! Maybe it's dinner, bowling, or just coffee, but go do it!

THE THREE QUESTIONS

This week, use Romans 12. Read through it and answer the questions.

1. What is God saying?

2. What is God calling me to do?

3. What is my next step?

CLOSING

Make sure you know when you are getting together next.

Pray for one another. Take prayer requests and close in prayer. Spread out the prayer requests so as many people are praying as are available.

BEFORE NEXT TIME

Read the "Follow" devotion and chapter 8, answer the questions for that chapter, and be prepared to share your three-question answers with the group!

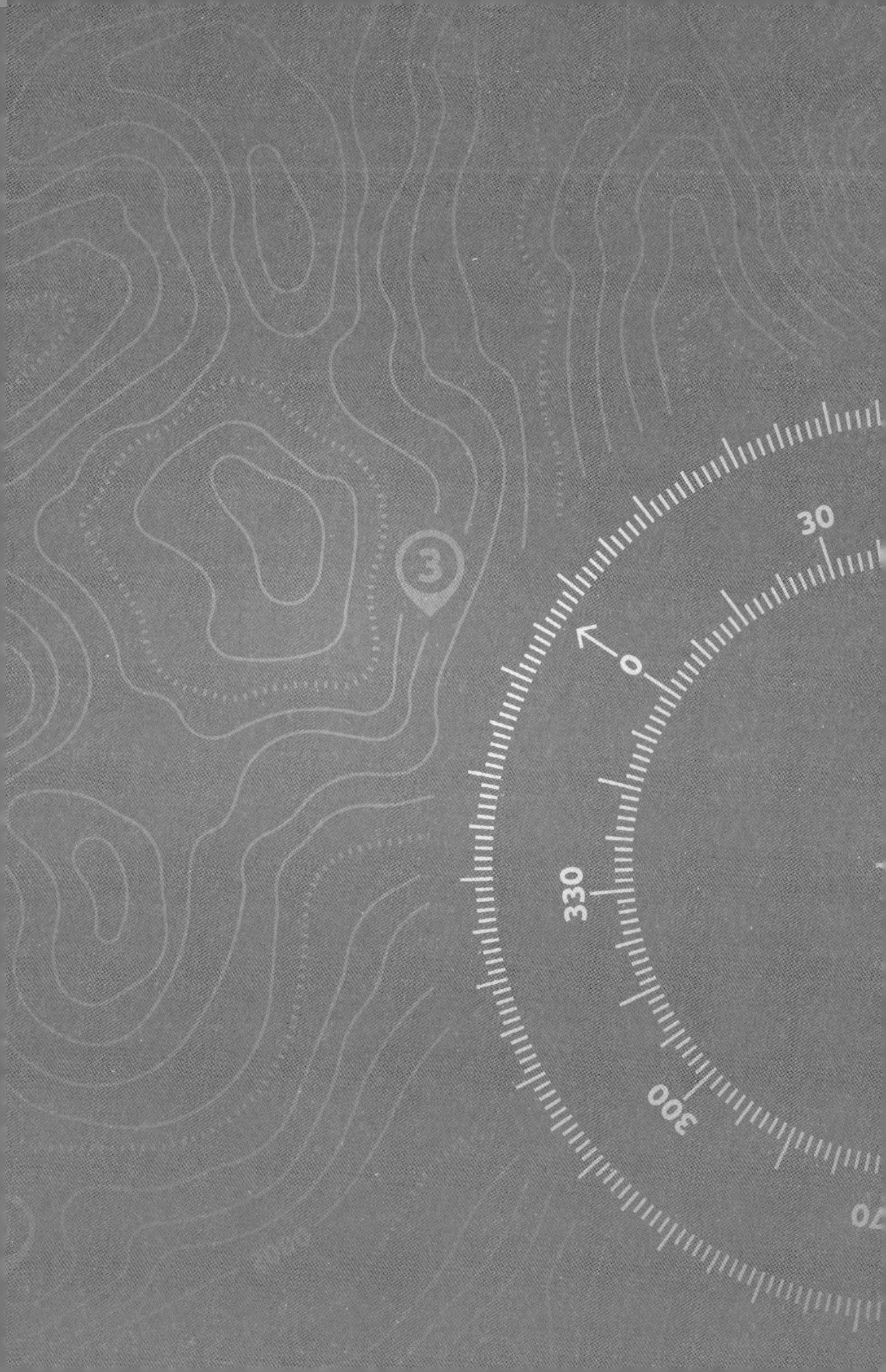
3
30
0
330
300

Follow

And they devoted themselves to the apostles' teaching and the fellowship, to the breaking of bread and the prayers. And awe came upon every soul, and many wonders and signs were being done through the apostles. And all who believed were together and had all things in common. And they were selling their possessions and belongings and distributing the proceeds to all, as any had need. And day by day, attending the temple together and breaking bread in their homes, they received their food with glad and generous hearts, praising God and having favor with all the people. And the Lord added to their number day by day those who were being saved.

Acts 2:42–47

The Book of Acts gives us an incredible view of what it means to follow Jesus. This was the first generation of disciples. Among them were the people who had heard Jesus speak and had followed Him through the countryside during His ministry. There are incredible stories of how these people followed Jesus after He had ascended.

Take a look at the verses above, especially the first two lines. You can learn a lot about following Jesus in those verses. Teaching, fellowship, eating, prayers—that was the focus of the first disciples. That's where it all started. Following Jesus is about action; stepping out of your door and doing the things that He taught you to do.

But what follows is interwoven with seeking and rooted in trusting. These three ideas cannot be separated. They are built to function together. Trusting Jesus leads you to seek Him, which then shows you the ways to follow Him.

What are some ways you follow Jesus in your life? Would you say that you are doing a good job of that right now? What are some ways you have seen people abuse the idea of following Jesus? Again, take time to discuss these questions with your group, sharing ideas and seeing what one another has to say about it.

Following Jesus is much simpler than we make it. But in that simplicity, you have to actually do it. There is no getting around the fact that following Jesus takes action. Even if that action is to rest, that is still an action. Seeking meant opening your Bible and being vulnerable. Following will mean taking that vulnerability and what you have heard from the Word of God out of your front door.

Take a moment to look at your life. What are some areas in which you need to follow Jesus? Is there a place He is calling you to go where you don't want to follow?

> Lord, give me strength to take what You have
> taught me and walk it into where You have
> placed me. May I be salt and light to a world

in need. May I see need and be Your hands and feet. Give me a heart that wants to help those who are less fortunate. Teach me to love my neighbor. Amen.

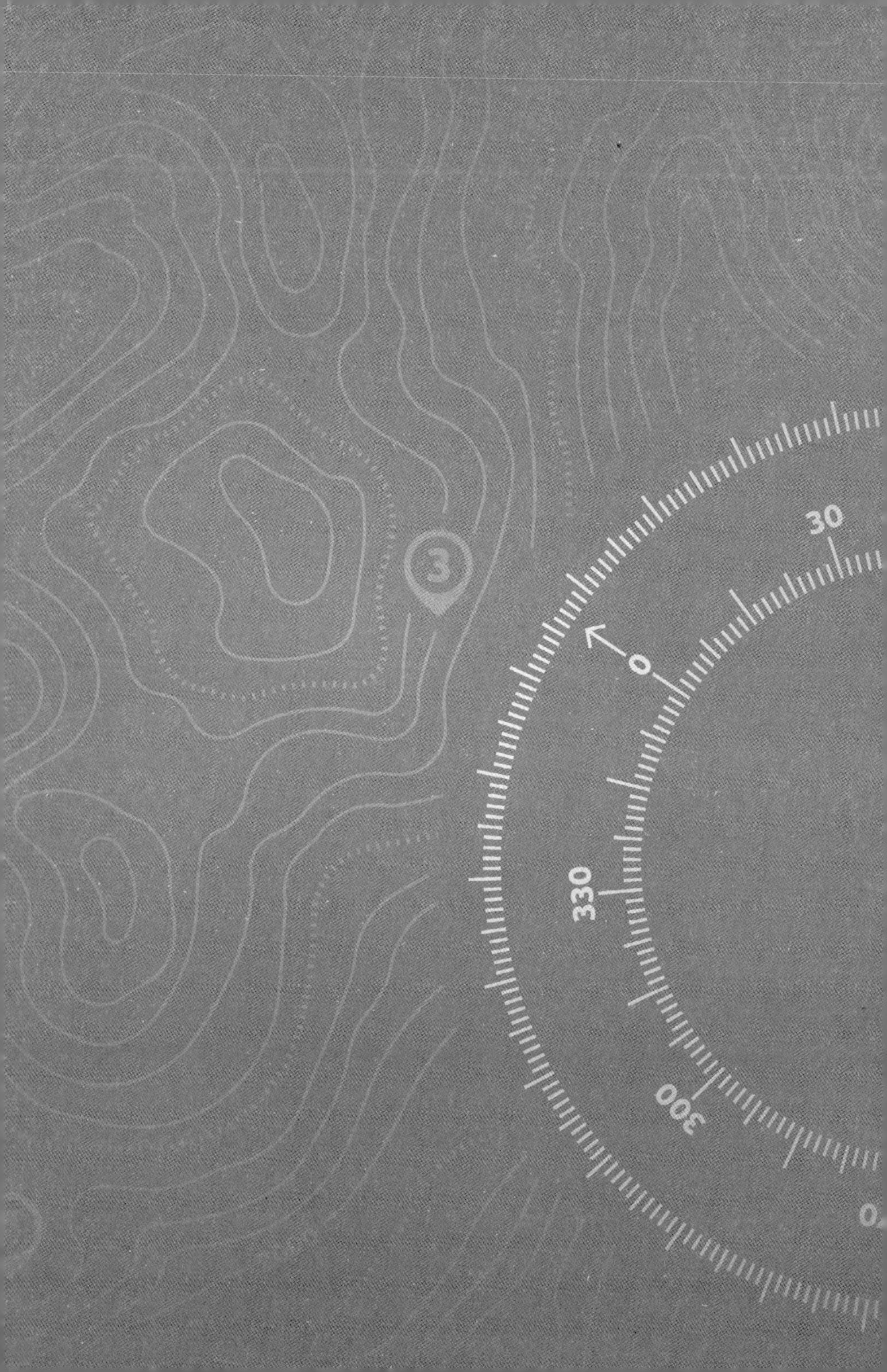
3
30
0
330
300

Prayer

In professional baseball, players take time at the beginning of the season and then before every game to work on the fundamentals. Pitchers work on arm mechanics and specific grips for different pitches. Fielders take grounders and pop-ups and run through fielding scenarios. Before every game, there is batting practice to get the logistics of a swing locked in and ready for the day. This isn't unique to baseball. Every sport has fundamentals that professionals practice over and over so that it becomes second nature.

This phenomenon doesn't exist only for sports either. Cooking, acting, singing, playing an instrument, physics, welding, carpentry—the list is never ending. All of them have fundamentals that are continually practiced so that they become second nature. When the fundamentals are nailed down, it is quick memory that pulls the trigger on more complex functions. And when fundamentals atrophy from lack of practice, every other function suffers.

Everything so far in this book could be viewed as fundamental. At the foundation, the promises of Jesus are our power and source of life. Worship, Sacraments, and hearing from God all form a structure for the life of us disciples. When they are lacking in our life, returning to them rebuilds a cornerstone element of faith. Another key element of that structure is prayer. Some people are given the gift of prayer. They can find quiet solitude and remain in prayer for hours. Others, when given time to pray, start looking at their watches within the first several minutes, thinking they have already hit their requests twice or more. But prayer is fundamental. It should not be ignored or laid to the side. Those who are gifted at prayer should continue to grow in it. They should regularly spend time learning how it works in their lives. Those who seek to grow but struggle will need to do the drills, to learn to make prayer a fast-twitch muscle in all situations. A Christian's life should be drenched in prayer.

The Fundamentals

If prayer is fundamental to the discipleship journey, then what are the fundamentals of prayer? Prayer is a strange idea that functions in incredible ways. Learning how to pray will be another lifelong endeavor of the disciple's journey. I don't know of anyone who just woke up one day and thought, "You know, I have a great prayer life. I can take a break today." Learning what prayer does and how to do it are meaningful steps in the right direction.

What Prayer Does

Do not be anxious about anything, but in everything by prayer and supplication with thanksgiving let your requests be made known to God. And the peace of God, which surpasses all understanding,

will guard your hearts and your minds in Christ
Jesus. (Philippians 4:6–7)

These verses from Philippians give us incredible insight
into the two major functions of prayer. Take a moment to read
through them again. First, they remind us that we are to take
everything to God in prayer. Prayer is our way of communicating with God. The omnipresent, all-knowing Creator of the
universe wants to talk to us. That continues to blow my mind
to this day. God surely has more important things to do than
spend time listening to what is going on in my life. And not
only does He make the time for us but He also wants to hear
it—even though He already knows it. He wants to listen and
hear from us. Second, when we bring our requests before God
in prayer, it changes us. Notice at the beginning of these verses
from Philippians that Paul calls us not to be anxious, to bring
everything before God, and *then* the peace of God will guard
our hearts and minds in Christ Jesus. Prayer is not just about us
taking our thoughts, fears, and requests before God. It is about
how He changes us as we do that.

God gives us access to Him. Pause and think about that.
The almighty Lord of heaven and earth, the Creator of it all, the
commander of the armies of the heavens, wants to hear how
your day is going. He wants you to bring to Him your fears,
requests, praises, and gratitude. Through Jesus, our great me-
diator, God wants us to take time with Him every day. He has
called us friend. This is an awe-filled task. Why would we be
deemed so worthy as to bring these things to God? Yet, in the
power of the redemption we receive through the Son, God calls
us closer to Him. This is the way we were created to be. Prayer

is the reflection of what Adam and Eve had in the Garden when they walked with God. They could see Him, talk to Him, hear His responses. This side of the second coming, we are given prayer as a gift where God says, "I want to be with you and know you." We can rest whatever we need upon Him. Look at how Scripture depicts this conversation:

> Thus says the LORD who made the earth, the LORD who formed it to establish it—the LORD is His name: Call to Me and I will answer you, and will tell you great and hidden things that you have not known. (Jeremiah 33:2–3)

> O LORD, I call upon You; hasten to me! Give ear to my voice when I call to You! Let my prayer be counted as incense before You, and the lifting up of my hands as the evening sacrifice! (Psalm 141:1–2)

> Rejoice always, pray without ceasing, give thanks in all circumstances; for this is the will of God in Christ Jesus for you. (1 Thessalonians 5:16–18)

> First of all, then, I urge that supplications, prayers, intercessions, and thanksgivings be made for all people, for kings and all who are in high positions, that we may lead a peaceful and quiet life, godly and dignified in every way. This is good, and it is pleasing in the sight of God our Savior, who desires all people to be saved and to come to the knowledge of the truth. For there is one God, and there is one mediator between God and men, the man Christ Jesus, who gave Himself as a ransom for all,

which is the testimony given at the proper time.
(1 Timothy 2:1–6)

Constantly we are called to be in prayer. In the relationship of discipleship, prayer connects us to the Creator in supernatural ways. He does not want us to go a day without being in prayer. It is His gift to us, and He wants us to use it.

As we build up this fundamental, investing in relationship with our Creator, it changes who we are. Prayer is a two-way street. As we seek after God, He works on our hearts. In fact, prayer is one of the things that will propel us to follow Jesus. The peace that passes understanding is part of our sanctification process. God works through prayer to change us. It is a beautiful mystery, but God works. There is no deep way to explain it. But work to build your prayer life, and watch what happens. The Holy Spirit works in that time and brings us peace and strength, and when that peace and strength works itself out in our lives, we find that those promises of Jesus are fueling us.

Prayer in our lives will change who we are. The promises of Jesus find deep footholds as we build a life of prayer. That is the beautiful mystery. A simple act of prayer and God works. He delivers peace, strength, and hope. He tells us whatever we ask will be ours. Instead of thinking of God as our genie granting us wishes, what if He was saying that as we pray, our hearts align with His heart, and as we ask, we ask for the things He has prepared for us?

> When the righteous cry for help, the LORD hears and delivers them out of all their troubles. (Psalm 34:17)

> But seek first the kingdom of God and His righteousness, and all these things will be added to you. (Matthew 6:33)

> And I tell you, ask, and it will be given to you; seek, and you will find; knock, and it will be opened to you. For everyone who asks receives, and the one who seeks finds, and to the one who knocks it will be opened. What father among you, if his son asks for a fish, will instead of a fish give him a serpent; or if he asks for an egg, will give him a scorpion? If you then, who are evil, know how to give good gifts to your children, how much more will the heavenly Father give the Holy Spirit to those who ask Him! (Luke 11:9–13)

> In that day you will ask nothing of Me. Truly, truly, I say to you, whatever you ask of the Father in My name, He will give it to you. Until now you have asked nothing in My name. Ask, and you will receive, that your joy may be full. (John 16:23–24)

Prayer is our connection with God, and it will change us, even in our asking.

How

Praying can seem like a daunting task. There is fear around saying or doing the wrong thing. Set that fear to the side. If you feel like you messed up in a prayer, immediately ask forgiveness. Problem solved. When diving into how to pray, you may be a seasoned veteran or a green newcomer. Both are great places to be. If the practice of prayer has been in your life for a long time, and especially if you are reading this book in a group, jot down in the margins some of the ways that have helped you to pray. Share them. People want to know how to grow in their prayer lives. If you are new, take a minute to jot down some of the ways in which you want to grow in prayer. Seek out one of those prayer veterans (if you can't find one, I guarantee your pastor knows who they are in your church because he is asking them for prayer). Live together in community, sharing the knowledge, application, and experience of prayer together.

The Lord's Prayer

And when you pray, you must not be like the hypocrites. For they love to stand and pray in the synagogues and at the street corners, that they may be seen by others. Truly, I say to you, they have received their reward. But when you pray, go into your room and shut the door and pray to your Father who is in secret. And your Father who sees in secret will reward you. And when you pray, do not heap up empty phrases as the Gentiles do, for they think that they will be heard for their many words. Do not be like them, for your Father knows what you need before you ask Him. Pray then like this: Our Father in heaven, hallowed be Your name. Your kingdom come, Your will be done, on earth as it is in heaven. Give us this day our daily bread, and forgive us our debts, as we also have forgiven our debtors. And lead us not into temptation, but deliver us from evil. For if you forgive others their trespasses, your heavenly Father will also forgive you, but if you do not forgive others their trespasses, neither will your Father forgive your trespasses. (Matthew 6:5–15)

When you are looking to pray, start with how Jesus taught us. The Lord's Prayer is the place to see how to pray. It gives us a flow for how to pray, a template that can be prayed again and again.

Jesus starts off by reminding His disciples that their prayers are not meant to bring them glory or attention. He tells them not to be like actors, hypocrites who are just putting on a show, but instead to pray in a hidden place where their pride and vanity are stripped away. This follows in the first part of this prayer, "Our Father in heaven, hallowed be Your name." In other words, remember who the Creator is. As you pray about His greatness and holy name, you are both honoring Him and reminding yourself of who God is. This is not some little voice in your head you are responding to. The ruler of the cosmos is currently connecting with you, so may His name be hallowed. Hallowing the name of God is remembering who He is as Creator. It is standing in awe of who He is.

Next, Jesus instructs His disciples to pray in the ways of His kingdom. Pray for the Kingdom to come. That you would see how the Lord is at work through His Word and His people in the world around you. As part of this, pray that you act how the King has commanded you to act. Put your anxiety on God. Pray that you would see His daily provision in your life. Let prayers of forgiveness flow from your lips. We are constantly in need of that forgiveness; may we always pray for it. Then, let us not forget to forgive. As members of the Kingdom, we forgive because we were first forgiven. Asking for the spiritual fortitude to forgive others is part of who we seek to be. Also, we pray that God would not lead us into temptation. If that phrasing trips you up, instead think of it as God leading you through temptation. There will be many things to tempt you along the road; Jesus knows that. The prayer of "Lead me not into temptation" is not saying that God will lead you there but saying that as He guides you, He would bring you through it. It is acknowledging the reality of the world while placing your hope in Jesus. We ask for delivery from evil and the evil one. Evil and darkness surround us, but God is greater than all of it.

Over the years, the Church has added a conclusion to the Lord's Prayer: "For Thine is the kingdom and the power and the glory forever and ever. Amen." This final phrase brings us back to the promises of Jesus. It references how the prayer started and focuses us as we end. We live in the Kingdom, but it is not our own; we are stewards of a mighty King. Our power does not come from ourselves but from the Creator. We do not seek our own glory but instead relish the fact that we get to bring glory to God until the end of time.

If you haven't already, memorize the Lord's Prayer. It is a gift of Jesus to His people: a simple prayer that covers all the points of how we can pray. In our times of need, it is there to comfort us, challenge us, and bring us into connection with God. What an amazing gift. Pray it daily. Physically slow down your cadence as you do to focus on the incredible things that you are saying in the prayer.

It was an incredible experience to sit with my grandmother and pray this prayer together. Toward the end, she couldn't remember our names, but when we started praying the Lord's Prayer, she was right there with us. This prayer is a blessing to the community of faith. Use it as often as you can.

Personal Prayer

The Lord's Prayer sets us up with an incredible template; it is the foundation on which we can build all prayer. Throughout Scripture, there are stories of prayer and the people of God engaging Him through it. David writes an entire book based on his prayer life. Daniel prays in the midst of the Babylonian captivity. Mary prays an incredible prayer when she finds out that she will bear Jesus. Jesus continually prays throughout the Gospels. Prayer is part of the daily life of the disciple. Prayer should incorporate praise of God, confession of sins and a request for forgiveness, community surrounding the disciple, requests that are on the heart, and thanksgiving for how God is at work in one's life.

As the Lord's Prayer demonstrates, personal prayer should include praise of God because it helps us see that prayer is a gift and connection that we do not deserve but are blessed to have. If you are struggling with the right wording, use Scripture. Here are two examples:

> In the beginning, God created the heavens and the earth. (Genesis 1:1)

> Have you not known? Have you not heard? The LORD is the everlasting God, the Creator of the

ends of the earth. He does not faint or grow weary;
His understanding is unsearchable. (Isaiah 40:28)

Bring it back to the amazing work of God in creation. Speak how unknowable He is. Connect that to His steadfast love. Praise Him for whatever reminds you that this great God would send His Son for you!

Confession should also be present in personal prayer. We have already discussed the importance of Confession and Absolution in the worship life of the Church. But daily confession in personal prayer leads us back to the foot of the cross. This is another way in which we access the promises of Jesus. Through this time, we bring our sins before God. While He knows everything about us and what we have done, our confession works both ways. It builds our relationship with Him and it works on our hearts. In our confession, He has promised to be faithful. There is forgiveness. Listing our sins is not an act of self-deprecation but instead of trusting that God will provide again and again. As we pray, confession changes us. It renews us because God provides His promise.

Confession in personal prayer is another piece of the head, heart, and hands connection:

By this is love perfected with us, so that we may have confidence for the day of judgment, because as He is so also are we in this world. There is no fear in love, but perfect love casts out fear. For fear has to do with punishment, and whoever fears has not been perfected in love. We love because He first loved us. (1 John 4:17–19)

How do we learn to love those around us? We remember that we were first loved by God. The quickest way to see that love is to confess our sins and trust the promises of forgiveness. Continual confession keeps in front of us the reality that we are sinners saved by grace. This knowledge works on our heart, driving into the core of our being. From there, it becomes part of how we live our lives, forgiving others because we are forgiven. Confessing in personal prayer leads us to a life of forgiveness, for ourselves and others.

Praying for community is another part of the disciple's prayer. Earlier in the book, we talked about worship as a time to recharge and be sent out into the week, back into the places where we live. Be in prayer for those places. Continually lift up your church in prayer. Keep the neighborhood where you live in prayer. Pray for the neighbors you know and the neighbors you don't. Ask some of those neighbors how you can be praying for them. That may be scary, but prayer is a powerful tool through which we can bless not only ourselves but also others. Pray for the place where you work. Pray for the places your kids attend school. Pray for your sports leagues, barbershop quartets, and favorite coffee shop. Blanket everywhere you go in prayer. "But seek the welfare of the city where I have sent you into exile, and pray to the LORD on its behalf, for in its welfare you will find your welfare" (Jeremiah 29:7).

What kind of requests should you bring before God as you pray? All of them. Healing, peace, strength, direction for yourself and for others—anything you might want to ask God, you should bring as a request to Him. These requests are about taking fear, anxiety, hope, strength, and weakness and laying them all before God. It shows our deep care for others and the struggles we are having ourselves. Making requests can be one of the hardest parts of prayer. It is definitely one of the most faith-filled ways in which to pray. God tells us we can ask for anything and, if we have faith, we will receive it. At times, we may feel as if we have no faith, as our prayers seem to go answered. Even when we are praying for the sick and downtrodden, those prayers may not be answered in the way we expect or wish. This is once again about learning to pray and seeing our heart changed in the midst of prayer. We won't always get the answer we are looking for when we pray. Sometimes we may not even see an answer. God is still good in the midst of it all. As we pray our requests, we constantly seek the will of God above our own. That is why, in our requests, we ask that God would do what is best, not what we think should happen.

Praying requests is an incredible tool that Jesus has given us to connect with others. As we follow Jesus, prayer will always be the way we start. It brings us back to the heart of God over and again. Following Jesus takes the step of discipleship out our front door to connect with the world around us. Prayer is an incredible way to do that, with both Christians and people who don't know Jesus. Just asking people what you can pray about for them has meaning. Christians, disconnected followers, and unbelievers hear your question, "Is there anything I can be praying for you?" and they see that you care about them. It is a straightforward question to ask a fellow Christian and yet one of the scariest to ask of someone you've just met. The next time you are at a restaurant, try this. After your order is taken, ask the waiter or cashier, depending on the restaurant, "Hey, we will be praying before we eat. Is there anything we can be praying about for you?" Use prayer as a tool to bless people. Let your time with God be about more than just yourself. See how the Spirit will work through that simple question.

Always give thanks in your prayers. One of the most frequent attacks of the enemy will be to draw your attention away from the gifts that God has given you. He will work to direct your gaze at the things you don't have or the areas of your life where there is struggle to make you feel discontent about as much as he can. Gratitude is a weapon in the disciple's tool kit. It is built to destroy discontentment and show the blessings that God has given to you. It's the least complicated process in the world. As you pray, think on the things that God has given you. Make a list before you pray, and then pray through your list. For the big blessings and the small, give thanks. Give thanks for the people in your life, for the meals you get to eat, for the things you have, and for whatever you spend your days doing. There will be seasons when it's harder to give thanks—at the loss of loved ones, when employment suddenly ends, when there is strife in relationship. Continue to give thanks as much as you can in the midst of these things. See how God uses thankfulness to work on your heart.

Praise, confession, community, requests, thanksgiving. Those are the pieces that make up personal prayer. Use them to build your prayer life. If prayer is a new practice for you, start small. Set aside a few minutes each day to be in prayer. Watch what God does through that time. If you have built a life of prayer, may this list encourage you as you continue on that journey. Share the practices that have benefited your life of prayer with those around you.

Look for ways to grow your prayer life. There are incredible resources that can help you as you grow. Prayer books help to put into words things that might be hard for you to say, and they can help build a daily rhythm for prayer. If you are looking to spend more time with the Lord's Prayer, both Luther's Small and Large Catechisms are helpful in finding more information. Investing in a journal or using the notes feature on your phone can be beneficial. Keep track of what you are praying so that you can come back and see how God is working in the midst of your prayers. Notes or a journal can also be helpful if you find yourself easily distracted while praying. Write down your prayers. The act of writing will keep you focused in one direction instead of having your thoughts pulled all over the place. As you write, you pray; and as you pray, you write.

The key thing is to do it. Pray. Personally, on your own, in a quiet place. Seek the Lord. Spend the time with Him that He is seeking from you. Watch how a personal life of prayer develops you as a disciple.

Praying Together

Praying privately is not the only form of prayer. The Body of Christ prays together. There is no doubt that this form of prayer adds to the bonds of the followers of Jesus. Whether it is a formal prayer during a church service or the prayers of a few gathered, the Church prays together.

Formalized prayers while gathered in worship are import-ant for the life of the believer, whether spoken by the pastor or worship leader or spoken by everyone gathered together. There is power in the Church coming together during worship and praying. It is amazing to see many people together praying and hearing the blessings of prayer and bringing their requests before God. Those prayers shared together are a personal appeal brought to the public Body. What an incredible gift of the community to be in prayer for one another, showing the care they have for one another. The prayers during the service also remind hearers of who God is and pull them back to the promises of Jesus, bringing together the Body of believers around our God and His attributes.

Another, less formalized way to share prayer together in the Body is simply by praying for one another together. This may take place in Bible studies and homes, among friends, family, and strangers. This prayer connects the Body together. Never miss an opportunity to pray for one another. When someone shares a struggle or a prayer request, work to change your response from "I will be praying for you" to "Can we pray for that right now?" It may seem strange to stop and pray immediately, but what a blessing it is to join together with fellow believers in connection with God! Continue to pray for that need (and follow up with that person if you can), but actually stopping in the moment to pray is a powerful way to show the deep love and compassion of Jesus to someone.

There is often a fear of praying out loud in a group. Most of the time this is because people feel as if they will say or do something wrong. God is not looking for flowing and flowery language; He is looking for conversation. If this is a struggle for you, work to overcome it. Return to the promises of Jesus. He is the one who has authority and power, and He has brought you into the family. Leading prayer with a group of people out loud may seem daunting, but Jesus is the one who gives you the authority to do so.

Prayer and Following Jesus

A disciple is someone who trusts the promises of Jesus and seeks to follow Him. The move from trusting and seeking to following, living out good works God created for you to do, is powered by prayer. Trusting the promises of Jesus is our source of life and power in the discipleship journey. Seeking after God shows us how we are being called to live out that journey. Following is putting that into action—head, heart, and hands. Prayer connects those areas of our lives. It takes the head knowledge of who God is, sinks it into our hearts, and pushes us out the door to live in this new way.

Following Jesus means we are praying and asking how we are to do that every day. As your feet hit the floor in the morning, pray a one-line simple prayer, "Lord, show me how to follow You today." It is that simple. So simple that you can pray it before you have your coffee! Because of the promises of Jesus, prayer changes our hearts. It changes our minds. It changes our actions. As we follow Jesus, prayer will propel us, connecting us to the Creator and showing us how He sees the world and the people around us. If you want to follow after Jesus, to walk in His ways, prayer will be the first step in connecting trusting and seeking with following.

If you struggle with prayer, your first step must be to start. Then remember the third question: what is your next step?

Work through that. Set up a plan to pray. Start small with the expectation that God is going to bless you as you go. Seek wisdom from those who have built a life of prayer; ask them how they do it. But do not live in research. Apply those things to your life. Build a life of prayer. Start today.

DISCIPLESHIP COMMUNITY

OPEN WITH PRAYER

Ask for a volunteer to open with prayer. Rotate who does this each time you get together. Praying in front of people may scare you, but it is worth growing in the practice. Praying together is part of what the Body of Christ does. Not only is it our connection to God but it also gives an example of how we live on this discipleship journey.

FROM LAST TIME

What are your answers for the three questions? How can we support you in your next step?

DISCUSSION

1. What jumps out to you in this chapter?

2. How would you rate your prayer life on a scale of 1 to 10?

3. Now that you have read the breakdown of the Lord's Prayer and have a personal prayer guide, what are some ways you can pray?

4. Anyone who ranks themselves as an 8 or higher on the scale, share tips and tricks to a healthy prayer life.

DO IT

Set aside time to pray. Share with the group how much time and how often you plan to pray over the next week.

THE THREE QUESTIONS

This week, focus on your previous next-step plans. Keep them going! Be ready to share next week.

CLOSING

Make sure you know when you are getting together next.

Pray for one another. Take prayer requests and close in prayer. Spread out the prayer requests so as many people are praying as are available.

BEFORE NEXT TIME

Read chapter 9 and be ready to share how your next steps are going and how prayer is working in your life!

Vocation

What does following Jesus look like in your everyday life? It's a simple question with a lifetime of answers. Discipleship, as we have discussed so far, is the process of figuring this out. You take in the knowledge of God and see who He is and what He does. It reveals that death was your birthright, but through the power of Jesus' work on the cross, you are now redeemed, made new, re-created in the waters of Baptism. That knowledge moves down to your soul, affecting and uniting the physical and spiritual. God has changed who you are because of His love for you. In the Old Testament, the word for that love is *chesed*. In the English Standard Version of the Bible, this is often translated as "steadfast love." A love that does not fade. God's love for you that—despite your sin—runs out to meet you wherever you are. When you combine knowledge with the application of God's *chesed* on your heart, you are moved to action. Paul wrote it to the Church in Ephesus like this:

> And you were dead in the trespasses and sins in which you once walked, following the course of this world, following the prince of the power of the air, the spirit that is now at work in the sons of disobedience—among whom we all once lived in the

passions of our flesh, carrying out the desires of the body and the mind, and were by nature children of wrath, like the rest of mankind. But God, being rich in mercy, because of the great love with which He loved us, even when we were dead in our trespasses, made us alive together with Christ—by grace you have been saved—and raised us up with Him and seated us with Him in the heavenly places in Christ Jesus, so that in the coming ages He might show the immeasurable riches of His grace in kindness toward us in Christ Jesus. For by grace you have been saved through faith. And this is not your own doing; it is the gift of God, not a result of works, so that no one may boast. For we are His workmanship, created in Christ Jesus for good works, which God prepared beforehand, that we should walk in them. (Ephesians 2:1–10)

Grace saves us. Nothing else. The unmerited work of Jesus for us. God's workmanship is once again made new and is sent into the world to do what we were created to do: the good works that He prepared for us beforehand. Now let's get big and bold about this up front: *These good works do not save you.* Instead, when the power comes from grace by faith, you walk in these good works. Following after Jesus means doing what He did as a reflection of Him, not as a carbon copy. You cannot take the sins of humanity to the cross. But you can sacrifice to show love to those around you. As the Holy Spirit works in your life, He will call you toward loving your neighbors.

Following Jesus . . . for Your Neighbor

As you follow Jesus in your life, the temptation will be to make it all about you. But there is freedom in vocation as a lens for serving your neighbor. Too often we can look at our world and ask, "What is in it for me?" With this idea, we evaluate where we shop, who we will be friends with, how we spend our time, and even what church we will attend. This idea isn't all bad. It isn't wrong to make sure there is benefit to us when we spend money or time. However, this can translate into how we follow Jesus. We look at all opportunities as we follow Him to be about our own personal needs. Will they be fulfilled if I do this task or activity? Slowly, our love of neighbor becomes a personal-growth issue. Instead of actually caring about people, we want to know what they can do for us or, even worse, we do a cost-benefit analysis of how we serve others. Caught up in the race of service, we forget who we are called to serve.

There is freedom in loving your neighbor for our neighbor's sake instead of what you might gain from it. When seeking to love others in obedience to the Word of God, don't lose sight of who those people are. There is temptation to make service beneficial to you, about how it brings your quotient of righteousness up or about how you must obey God for Him to love you more. Both of these things are solved at the cross. Your righteousness before God is made complete because of Jesus. God could not love you any more than He did when He sent Jesus to die for you. Loving your neighbor does not add to the righteousness that God sees when you are covered in the blood of Jesus.

Loving your neighbors in light of Jesus means that you get to love them for *their* sake. You do not need to change them.

That is the work of the Holy Spirit and not your job. You don't need to be their savior. That is the work of Jesus and not your job. Instead, you are called to serve and love them as fits you best. When Jesus tells us that His yoke is easy and His burden is light, this is part of what that means. We are not responsible for the salvation of others. We are not responsible for their behavior. Instead, we are called to be servants to all and look for ways to care for others because it is what God has called us to do.

Good works are not an obligation from God in order for Him to love us. God simply uses them to bless the world through us. God's plan has always remained the same. He first created Adam and Eve, molded in His own image, to bless the earth. God created humans as His image bearers and to steward the creation He built. Even after the descent into sin, that did not change. The role of humanity is not thrown to the side because of sin. It must simply be rediscovered. Believing that our good works are part of some divine scale helping us to reach God will be weighty. It will pull us down as works-righteousness consumes us. This is a slavery to good works that becomes self-focused garbage.

When our works become our salvation, it is like finding the most beautiful body of water with a perfect beach but then going in to swim covered in weights. The only way to survive is to try to tread water long enough to keep your breath and hopefully make it to shore.

When our works become about loving our neighbor, those weights are gone. Instead of struggling to swim, we are removing the barriers for our friends, family, and neighbors to join us at the beach. It is inviting them to be a part of the process.

It may take some time to let this sink in and rework how we view our good works. God does not need our good works, but still He created us to carry them out. We do not need our good works; our salvation is secure. Our neighbors need our good works. They need them to be encouraged, to know they are not alone, and to see God at work in our lives. The good works of disciples following Jesus give us a glimpse of the kingdom of God. It shows the ways of a Kingdom where the King declares that He has come to serve and not to be served. A Kingdom where the first shall be last and the last shall be first. A Kingdom of the Servant King. And if the King lives in this way, then so, too, do His people.

Part of this process is learning to reframe the question of following Jesus. Often, we seek out the *why* of situations. Whether it is a decision with small outcomes or one that will change our world, we go to God and ask questions centered on *why*. This is our human nature and curiosity. It is not wrong. But we do have to realize that we may not ever know the reasons why, or that time might be the way in which we learn the answers. Framing our questions around the idea of *what* can be more fruitful. *What* needs can I meet here? *What* does my neighbor need to see the love of God? *What* is my next step to love God and love my neighbor? We may never know the *why*, but we can step into the *what* of loving God and loving our neighbors wherever we are.

Just look at the story of Joseph. Joseph has some dreams and tells them to his brothers. He says that they, as the older brothers, will bow to him. In perfect older brother fashion, they throw him into a pit and then sell him into slavery because there is no way their little brother will rule over them. They take their brother's blood-soaked coat to their father and claim he has died. Sold by the slave traders to a family in Egypt, Joseph goes from slave to valued leader of the household. But the wife of the home accuses Joseph of untoward advances, even though she actually instigated the situation and Joseph fled from the scene. He is thrown in prison. While there, he ends up interpreting some dreams of Pharaoh's servants. When those prisoners are brought up before Pharaoh, who has himself been having disturbing dreams, one suggests Joseph as the man with the answers. Joseph interprets Pharaoh's dream and is put in charge of preparing Egypt for an oncoming famine. When the famine hits the land, Joseph's family is affected as well. His brothers—yes, the very ones who sold him into slavery—come to Egypt to barter for food because they heard that it was well stocked. Through a series of events, the brothers are brought before Joseph, and he finally reveals himself to them. After the shock and many discussions about whether they will die, the brothers bring their father to Egypt, and the Egyptians give the family fertile land to live on and raise their crops and livestock.

Throughout this story, we find Joseph doing *what* the people of God are called to do. This is before the exodus, before God gave His Law, yet here we find Joseph loving God and his neighbors. He isn't perfect; he might have tried to find a way not to gloat about his brothers worshiping him. But he seeks God in it all. From the pit of the hole to the highest position in Egypt second only to Pharaoh, Joseph continually searches for *what* God is calling him to do in the midst of where he is.

Your story may not be as extraordinary as Joseph's. In fact, there is a high chance that it will not be. But that doesn't mean that you don't seek *what* God is calling you to do in the places you live. Vocation is a blessing because you don't have to search for a deeper why to follow Jesus. Wherever you go, *what* do you do to love God and love your neighbor?

As You Go

Vocation gives you permission to follow Jesus in simple ways. There is a tendency as people of God to think we cannot do anything until we see a clear sign of what He is saying. But it is right there in His Word. Love God and love your neighbors. Vocation allows us to experience that every day. We don't have to ask for some grand sign or wait patiently to know what it means to love our neighbors. It means looking around us and loving those people who are in proximity as we go about our daily lives. This takes place in our homes, our neighborhoods, the places we work, and where we spend our free time.

At Home

When I do premarital counseling with couples, I always have them take a quiz to discover the ranking of their love languages. Discussion around the five love language ideas opens up opportunities for discovery of how to love and care for each other. Sometimes this is because the way one partner feels the communication of love is vastly different from the other. I know this is helpful, because it helped me. My wife is an incredible woman, and one of her chief love languages is service. She communicates love through serving others, taking care of them, keeping things neat and organized, and feeding them. Her family has a knack for hospitality that is God-given. It took me an embarrassingly long time to realize that if I wanted to communicate how much I loved her, the quickest way I could do it was to do the dishes. In just fifteen to twenty minutes, I can give my wife a tangible way to see that I love her. I would love to say I figured this out in the first year, or five, of our marriage. Over time I began to see that when I served her, she connected with the love I had for her and in turn with the love of God in that moment.

This is not a story about how great I am as a husband. The dishes are simple, and it took me years to figure out how serving communicated love. No, this is about how doing simple things shows love for God and love for our neighbors. It had stared me in the face for a long time. All I had to do was the dishes. I didn't need to try to figure out some elaborate way to communicate the love of God to my wife. I just needed to do the dishes. The first place we get to experience following Jesus and loving our neighbors is right where we live.

Living situations vary depending on stage of life and circumstances. Maybe you have a home full of children. Perhaps you are just out of college living with roommates. Or your children are all grown, and you live as an empty nester. Maybe you have established yourself as a single person and are navigating a world that seems built for families. Whatever your circumstances, home is where vocation begins.

Home is the central hub for where you spend your time. While it may not be where you spend the most waking time, it is the place where you lay your head. What are the ways in which you love God and love your neighbor there? This includes husbands, wives, mothers, fathers, sisters, brothers, roommates, and the like. The home is a fertile ground to begin the process of living out the ways of Jesus as you follow Him.

In Your Neighborhood

Do you know your neighbors—the people on the other side of the fence or the road or one apartment over? How many of the people in your group know their neighbors? In my experience, it's become pretty rare. But God has put you in your neighborhood with purpose. How do I know this? Wherever you go, Jesus is there. Once again, it would be tempting to sit and wait to try to find a reason for why God has put you there. But instead, what if you changed the questions from *why* to *what*? Instead of asking God to reveal to you *why* you are where you are, begin asking *what* you can do to love God and love others in your neighborhood.

The fact that you live where you do is enough reason to know that God has called you there. Stop looking at *why*. Look for *what*. *What* does your neighborhood need? *What* are ways you can love your next-door neighbors? Bringing in trash cans after trash day, helping with yard work when needed, or the simplest form: getting to know their names. How would your love for your neighbors, your physical neighbors, transform if you simply learned their names?

God has put you in this place with purpose. Stop searching for reasons outside of the simplest one: it is where you are. Jesus has already been working in that place. He has gone ahead to prepare it. But now you live there, a representative of the kingdom of God. How, then, do you love your physical neighborhood? Be a good neighbor. Don't get lost in petty arguments, and keep up with your trash can. Learn the names of the families. Spend time hearing the stories of people around you. Love them by taking care of your house. Care for the people around you. Show them the love of Jesus that dwells in you.

At Work

Jesus is at work where you work! Or go to school. Even at the place you take your kids for playdates. Whether you are building your dog-walking business or teaching calculus, the beauty of vocation is that it is where God has placed you. The Christian faith does not see one job as better than others. That is human temptation, to rank different employment as greater or worse. In the kingdom of God, a job is a means to an end. Being productive helps us feel a sense of purpose and fulfillment, but any job or work we do is really an opportunity to live out love for God and love for others.

You might work in a place that is open to your faith. Rejoice! What an incredible blessing. However, another person's workplace may be less open to expressions of religion. That still doesn't change the question. It is not *why* do you work in that place, but *what* and *who* God is calling you to love in that place. Start looking at that the *what*. Whether you are the leader of the workplace or the most recent hire, as a disciple, your question will always remain, "*What* is Jesus calling me to do here?" Do your work in such a way that it shows your love of God and love of neighbor. In fact, you don't have to be overtly "Christian" about it. Just do your work to the best of your ability. If your work is caring for your family and children, then do it as best you can. Are you a professional violinist? Then play that violin in such a way that it honors God! Do you own the local hardware store? Run your business in such a way that it is the best it can be and treat your customers fairly. Are you a pizza delivery driver? Make sure your cargo makes it on time and hot. This is a confession of who Jesus is in our work. We follow Him by doing the best we can, growing in our profession, and learning from our mistakes, wherever that work takes place. Our goal is to watch what the Lord will do when we seek to follow Him in excellence.

Vocation as Confession

You are the salt of the earth, but if salt has lost its taste, how shall its saltiness be restored? It is no longer good for anything except to be thrown out and trampled under people's feet. You are the light of the world. A city set on a hill cannot be hidden. Nor do people light a lamp and put it under a basket, but on a stand, and it gives light to all in the house. In the same way, let your light shine before others, so that they may see your good works and give glory to your Father who is in heaven. (Matthew 5:13–16)

How we act in the world is part of our confession of who Jesus is. Do not hide the light. Don't lose your saltiness. Following Jesus into the real world is an everyday endeavor. It is simple. Keep asking yourself *what*: *What* good can I do? *What* people are in need of help? *What* do I need to repent of *not* doing? Remember, the fuel for following Jesus is His promises.

You are not working to try to impress God with your actions. There isn't some deity battery you are filling up to help God by doing good. You are obeying the commands of Jesus to see the Kingdom shine a little bit into the world. By your actions, you confess who God is.

As Christians, moving from words to actions is hard. Yet, God created us to be a people of knowledge, talk, and action—head to the heart, heart to the hands. The enemy will constantly seek to pull us away from that good. The lie we have been told is that study and discussion are enough. But God is a God of action. He is the one who invites us on this journey to follow Jesus. There will be a push and pull in our lives like the moon on the tides. There will be days when, either willingly or unwillingly, we will follow Jesus. That morning, we will wake up and find that following Him is something that we can do because of the power He has given us. Other days, our sinful self will resurface, calling us back to the old sins we had hoped were in our past. Sometimes you can have both in one day. Even in the span of five minutes. This is why we discussed the importance of worship, the Body of Christ, and confession. Do not walk into the world as one who is already perfected. It will cause you to lose compassion and kindness for others. Instead, the journey of following Jesus is full of one simple confession: His grace is sufficient.

Sufficient to cover all my sins.

Sufficient to give me the power and authority to walk as an ambassador for the kingdom of God.

Sufficient to be a people of repentance, not of arrogance.

Sufficient to walk in both truth and grace.

The way in which we live confesses who Jesus is. That means that we love our neighbors in all that we do. That means that when we fail, we confess through repentance, both seeking and giving forgiveness. It means we seek all the fruit of the Spirit, not just the ones we like. Our confession is tied to both our words and actions. The Holy Spirit uses that confession to work on the hearts of those around us.

Let's jump back to the story of Joseph. Look at how his adopted nation reacted when his brothers returned and he was finally reunited with his family:

> When the report was heard in Pharaoh's house, "Joseph's brothers have come," it pleased Pharaoh and his servants. And Pharaoh said to Joseph, "Say to your brothers, 'Do this: load your beasts and go back to the land of Canaan, and take your father and your households, and come to me, and I will give you the best of the land of Egypt, and you shall eat the fat of the land.' And you, Joseph, are commanded to say, 'Do this: take wagons from the land of Egypt for your little ones and for your wives, and bring your father, and come. Have no concern for your goods, for the best of all the land of Egypt is yours.'" (Genesis 45:16–20)

Through his vocation, Joseph had blessed his adoptive country. He had loved God through it all and he had loved his neighbors in Egypt, whoever they were. Look at the regard Egypt had for Joseph. Pharaoh and his servants were pleased when Joseph reunited with his family. Pharaoh gave Joseph prime land for him and his family. Joseph's confession of who

God is impacted those around him. This was all in God's working, and it is worked out through every day following.

Time might be another piece of this confession. Discipleship is following God over a lifetime while seeking the Kingdom. Look at the story of Joseph again. Sold into slavery, believed dead by his father, he makes it into a decent house in Egypt only to be thrown in prison because of false accusations. Finally, he becomes the regent of Egypt. But when his brothers return, they fear him because they are afraid he will punish them. Joseph constantly reminds them that they are safe; he has forgiven them. Even years later, after their father dies, the brothers come before him fearing his retribution because they no longer have protection. Look at what Joseph says to them:

> But Joseph said to them, "Do not fear, for am I
> in the place of God? As for you, you meant evil
> against me, but God meant it for good, to bring
> it about that many people should be kept alive, as
> they are today. So do not fear; I will provide for you
> and your little ones." Thus he comforted them and
> spoke kindly to them. (Genesis 50:19–21)

That clarity could come only through trusting God over time. Joseph sees the *why* because he can finally see the whole picture. Following Jesus will mean you don't always get the answer to the question of *why*? right away. It will mean that you may have to wait a lifetime to see *why* you are loving your neighbors. Know that you are in the company of a long line of saints who have done the same thing.

Following Jesus could also bring you to places you don't want to go. John the Baptist followed God in all he did, yet he was executed. There is a long list of martyrs who followed Jesus and it led to their deaths. That is one way in which God calls His people. But that does not mean we do not follow. Living in vocation means that wherever God has placed us, we live as He has called us.

The Extraordinary

Following Jesus is simple: love God, love others. But it is also hard. Those two commandments will bring you joy and pain as you follow. There will be times you will rejoice as you see growth in yourself and Jesus at work. And there will be times when repentance will need to be on your lips as you fail once again and need the healing spring of the Gospel. So far, we have looked at how vocation works in daily life—in your home, neighborhood, and where you work. But this does not mean that you are off the hook for God working the extraordinary in your life through vocation. You should always be looking at where you are to love God and love your neighbors, but there will also be times when God will bring you to a place where He will call you to more, the *extra*-ordinary. As you trust and seek Jesus, following Him will mean that you might be led to places outside of your ordinary rhythms. Caring for the poor, sick, and marginalized. Joining in a Gospel mission around you. Taking on a great role in loving a neighbor who is in need. This is the *extra*-ordinary. It does not lead you outside of what God has called you to do; it is and should become part of your ordinary life. It is extra because God is calling you to more.

There will be tension between finding your limits and following Jesus. Guilt and shame have been used in the past as a bludgeon to tell people to do more. This is not that. This is listening to and hearing God as you trust and seek Him. You see His care for this world and see where Jesus is calling you to follow. It may mean more, but it is more given by a God who understands who you are and your limits. Also, you don't have to take on every project or every need. When Jesus sent out seventy-two disciples into the countryside, He told them that when they come upon a house and find a person who is peaceful, they should remain there. You won't do everything. But you will find those places of peace where Jesus has already prepared the way; follow Him.

God answers the question of *why* with His people. When there is suffering and hurt, He sends His Church, His redeemed, Kingdom people, into the world to be salt and light. They walk the everyday paths of homes, apartments, offices, schools, and sports fields. Following in the footsteps of their Savior, they seek to be stewards of the message given to them. Wherever they go, they seek to love God and confess Him through their actions to their neighbors. When they fail, they repent. When Jesus places a need in their way, they ask what they can do to help, how they can bring a small glimpse of the kingdom of God into this world.

You are one of these Kingdom people. Look around you. Start asking *what* instead of *why*. *What* is Jesus calling me to do in this place? *What* are needs I can address? *What* is my next step? Citizenship in the Kingdom is purchased through Jesus' work on the cross, and life as a Kingdom steward is granted through the empty tomb. The King is reigning, and He invites you to be a part of spreading the Kingdom. Changing diapers, picking up trash, feeding the poor, doing the dishes, building homes for the homeless—these are all Kingdom tasks. Do not fall into the lie that you must be working some high-level ministry task to be doing Kingdom work. Never allow your fear to keep you from extraordinary callings of God to love Him and your neighbors. *What* is the King calling you to do to follow Him today?

OPEN WITH PRAYER

Ask for a volunteer to open with prayer. Rotate who does this each time you get together. Praying in front of people may scare you, but it is worth growing in the practice. Praying together is part of what the Body of Christ does. Not only is it our connection to God but it also gives an example of how we live on this discipleship journey.

FROM LAST TIME

How are your next steps going? How did your time in prayer go? How is God working on your heart?

DISCUSSION

1. What jumped out to you in this chapter?

2. What are some of your vocations?

3. How does living in your vocations encourage every-day discipleship?

4. Who are your neighbors? What are some ways God is calling you to love these people?

DO IT

Make a plan to love neighbors together. Keep it simple, but find a way to serve others!

THE THREE QUESTIONS

As a group, read through Mark 12:28–34 during your discussion time. Have each person walk through his or her answers to the three questions as they relate to those verses.

1. What is God saying?

2. What is He calling me to do?

3. What is my next step?

CLOSING

Make sure you know when you are getting together next.

Pray for one another. Take prayer requests and close in prayer. Spread out the prayer requests so as many people are praying as are available.

BEFORE NEXT TIME

Read chapter 10, answer the questions for that chapter, and be prepared to share how your next step for Mark 12:28–34 is going!

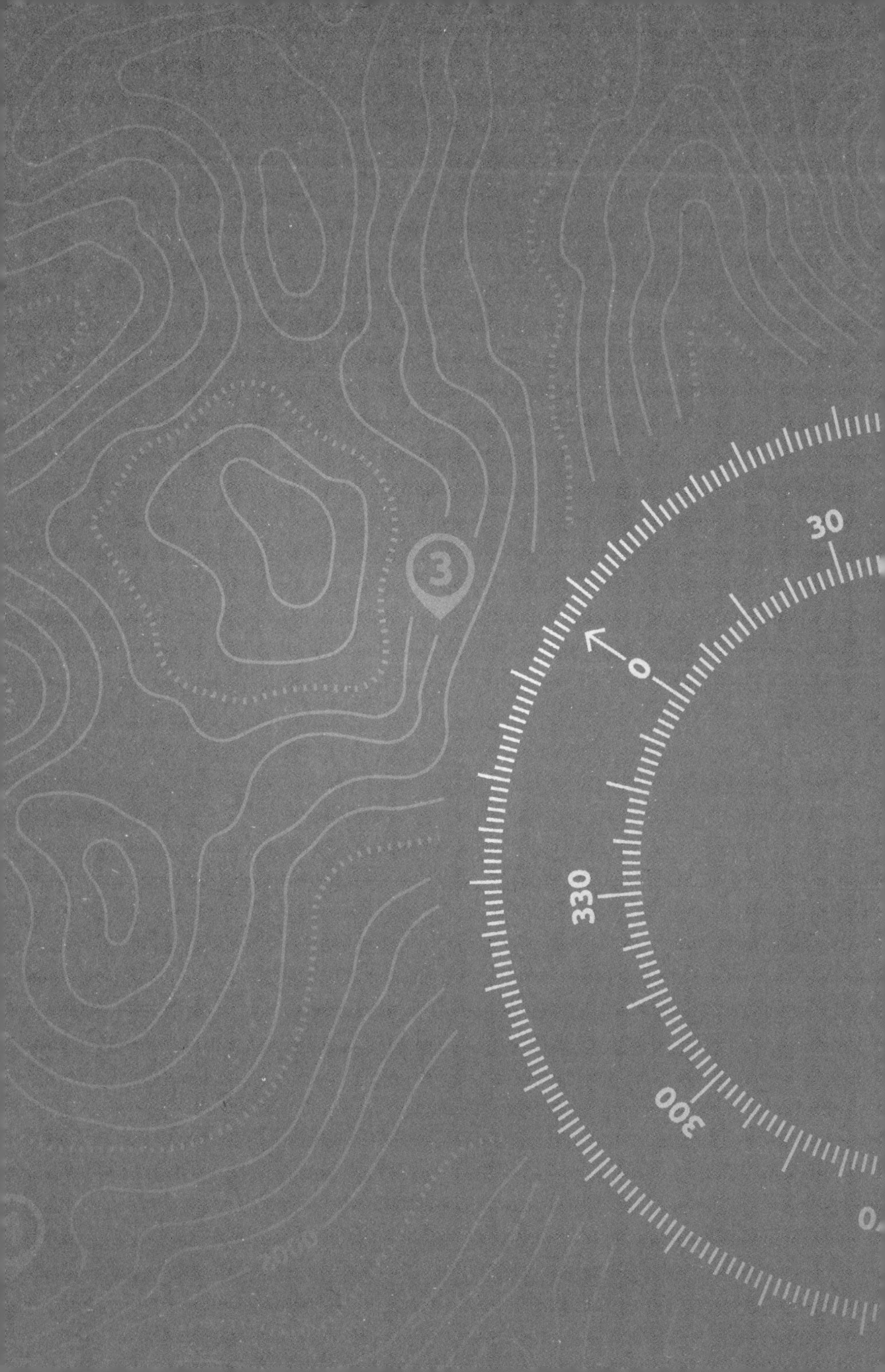
3
30
0
330
300

Story

If I close my eyes and think about it, I can still smell the pepperoni pizza. Little eight-year-old me was getting a treat. My mom had taken my brother and sister on a trip to visit family in Minnesota. We rotated years who got to go, and my brother was still young enough to go each time. That meant I got a fun week at home with Dad. We did all kinds of exciting things. Camping, fishing, hanging out. But there was one night he had a meeting at church—he's a pastor—and that meant I got to hang out in a classroom with my pizza and a movie. This was still in the days when we went to Blockbuster to rent a VHS tape. Being an only child for a short moment meant that, for once, I got to choose the movie without any discussion. Except for one problem. Walking the aisles with so many choices, my dad stopped suddenly, picked up a movie, and said, "This is the one for tonight. You'll have to trust me." Considering he was both buying my pizza and renting my movie, I didn't put up much of a fuss.

I was set up in a small classroom just off the big meeting room in the family life center. Dad rolled in the TV cart, double-checked to make sure the VCR was working properly, poured me a soft drink, handed me the remote, and then closed the door behind him as he started his meeting. All set, I pushed

Play. Blue letters popped onto the screen: "A long time ago in a galaxy far, far away . . ." My life was changed. I spent the next two hours having my mind blown by *Star Wars: A New Hope*. The classic story of good versus evil. A farm boy takes on the galaxy. My eight-year-old imagination was lit on fire.

Story is a central piece of what it means to be human. While my story is about *Star Wars*, think back to your childhood. What story jumps out to you? Maybe it was a book you read, a play you saw, or a song you heard. It could've been a feature on an Olympic athlete, telling the story of how he or she had trained and overcome adversity to stand on the podium. Story is a key part of what pulls on our hearts.

Weaving its way throughout Scripture is the greatest narrative we could ever encounter. It has all the aspects of an incredible story. Authors over the years have used the themes of God's Word to write entire fantastical worlds. Musicians hear the great story of the Savior and compose some of the greatest works of instrumentation and voice the world has ever known. Poets and artists follow suit. The stories found in Scripture work together to tell an overall narrative of a God who so deeply loved His creation that He would sacrifice His Son for it. Not only that, but that Son would rise again to conquer death and give new life to His people, inviting them to live as people of the Kingdom wherever they go.

Jesus is calling you to share who He is with others. Both unbelievers and those in the faith need to hear what Jesus is doing in your life. This is another way of loving your neighbor. It is the greatest way to love your neighbor. Your actions through vocation give you a voice to share this story.

Storytelling will be part of your discipleship journey. Learning how to share who Jesus is and what He is doing in your life is an incredible gift as you follow Him. This is often one of the scariest parts of the journey. Many people believe that they do not know enough or that they will become tongue-tied when they speak up about Jesus. Multiple times I have heard people say, "I want to learn how to talk about Jesus to my friends without looking weird." It is too important for you to simply lay this idea to the side. You are part of the story of Jesus; you just need to learn how to become a storyteller.

How

Storytelling can live solely in the realm of theory, but Jesus' story must enter your reality. You are blessed and called to be a follower of Jesus. His followers tell His story, just as He did. Wherever He went, He told the story of the Kingdom. Through His teaching, parables, and miracles, Jesus brought light into a dark world. But how do you emulate Jesus as a storyteller? How do you follow Him in this way? Remember these things: you aren't the hero; know your audience; and tell the story free of shame.

YOU'RE NOT THE HERO

Jesus is the hero of this story. No one else can have that place. Do not try to make yourself the center of the tale. Knowing you are not the hero is key to your storytelling, but it's also freeing for you. Christians do not need to be the center of their story, even as they tell it. Instead, share an honest and authentic story of who you are and what Jesus is doing in your life. Don't mix up who the main character is.

You need a hero. Coming back around to Law and Gospel, along with Confession and Absolution, we constantly remind ourselves that we will fail. Our hero, the one who will never fail, is Jesus. When we seek to become the main character of our stories, we invite pride to take center stage. Pride will lead us to ruin. If you want to see a story about following Jesus fall apart, put yourself in as the hero.

There is freedom when you aren't the focus of the story. Christians can fall into a sense of guilt when they feel like they must be the one to save the world. There will always be issues in the world that need the focus of the Kingdom. But you are not the one saving the world. That is Jesus' job. Live in freedom because you get to tell the story of the King.

Now, the amazing thing is that you get to share how the King enters your life. In your Baptism, God claimed you. He stretched down from heaven and said, "You. You are Mine." Not only does He choose you but He even makes you a part of the family. He calls you a friend. Let that sink in for a moment. You aren't a part of the Kingdom simply peeking in at the party go- ing on inside. You are a member of the family. Jesus saved you. Jesus came for you! You! The whole world and also specifically you. Paul eloquently proclaims it in Romans 5:6: "For while we were still weak, at the right time Christ died for the ungodly." Jesus didn't come when you had your act together. He didn't come for you when you finally solved that one sin that keeps pestering you. No. He came for you as you are. There is nothing you have done and nothing you will do that can separate you from His love. Nothing.

> What then shall we say to these things? If God is for us, who can be against us? He who did not spare His own Son but gave Him up for us all, how will He not also with Him graciously give us all things? . . . Who shall separate us from the love of Christ? Shall tribulation, or distress, or persecution, or famine, or nakedness, or danger, or sword? . . . No, in all these things we are more than conquerors through Him who loved us. For I am sure that neither death nor life, nor angels nor rulers, nor things present nor things to come, nor powers, nor height nor depth, nor anything else in all creation, will be able to separate us from the love of God in Christ Jesus our Lord. (Romans 8:31–32, 35, 37–39)

Nothing separates us from the love we have in Christ Jesus. That is the cornerstone of your story. Nothing takes the place of that. "We preach Christ crucified, a stumbling block to Jews and folly to Gentiles" (1 Corinthians 1:23). That is the central idea. Jesus is the hero. Let nothing take that place of honor. Your story is not about how great you are, not about "Look at the things I've done because God has somehow brought me into my destiny." No, your story is about how God is so good that He would send His Son for you and how that one fact has turned your life on its head and is daily changing you.

This is always where your story begins. This is where your story ends.

KNOW YOUR AUDIENCE

Too often we think that some rote, scripted, robotic response will connect with people. When was the last time you got a call from a telemarketer or a political campaign worker who, though reading off a prewritten script, connected with you enough that you didn't hang up right away? That is unlikely to have ever happened. Why, then, do we have the idea that we will change people if only we can say the right combination of words in the right way? Our stories are not magic incantations. Our stories tell of a real-life Savior who steps into our world. Understanding who you are talking to will inform how you tell your story.

Those Outside

> But in your hearts honor Christ the Lord as holy, always being prepared to make a defense to anyone who asks you for a reason for the hope that is in you; yet do it with gentleness and respect. (1 Peter 3:15)

Connecting with those outside the Church will be much different from connecting with those within. We use a certain language when communicating with others in the Church. We know the way to speak about Scripture, doctrine, and daily faith life. But to those outside, those words may take, at the very least, extra explanation. As you relate the story of Jesus to those outside of the faith, remember that they do not know what you know. Adjust your story accordingly to help them understand and connect.

Stand firmly in the knowledge that you do not cause the conversion or faith of another person. That work sits firmly in the hands of the Holy Spirit—again, another aspect of freedom. While there should be preparation for connecting with people who don't trust Jesus, remember that you are not in control. The Holy Spirit is the one who makes the work happen. He is working through you but is not dependent on you. In fact, He will give you the things to say: "And when they bring you before the synagogues and the rulers and the authorities, do not be anxious about how you should defend yourself or what you should say, for the Holy Spirit will teach you in that very hour what you ought to say" (Luke 12:11–12). Don't live in guilt or fear. Instead, live as a storyteller of Jesus and trust the Holy Spirit to work.

Trust the Spirit; know the story. The Spirit will work in you, but He has given you the gift of being able to read and comprehend the Scriptures. Spend time getting to know the Word and how it works in your life. Seek to understand who Jesus is so that you can tell His story all the more clearly. Remember, God works through everyday means. He works through you. The Holy Spirit will continue to work, but you have been given the very Word of God. Do not neglect it. A good storyteller knows the source material.

As you tell the story of Jesus, know that it will probably sound weird to unbelievers. You believe that a first-century Middle Eastern carpenter is in fact the Son of God, that He has taught His people how to follow Him to this day, and that He died and rose again. That's weird. There is no getting around it. But faith manifests itself as belief in things that seem unbelievable. Accepting this fact will help you to tell the story of Jesus in your life. It is another aspect of trusting Jesus: "For as the rain and the snow come down from heaven and do not return there but water the earth, making it bring forth and sprout, giving seed to the sower and bread to the eater, so shall My word be that goes out from My mouth; it shall not return to Me empty, but it shall accomplish that which I purpose, and shall succeed in the thing for which I sent it" (Isaiah 55:10–11). God works in the weird. His Word will do what He wants it to as it goes out.

What you should seek to do is not be a jerk. Peter tells us to have a defense for the hope in us (1 Peter 3:15). But we should give that defense of hope with gentleness and respect. Temptation has always existed to try to prove people wrong and guilt them into belief. Learning to share that defense without being defensive might be the most nuanced part of sharing your faith. You may not be perfect in this, but seek to be kind. The goal is not to prove someone wrong but to tell the person the story of the Savior. The nuance, and a lifelong pursuit of the disciple, is how to let your story share the need for a Savior. Sin is sin; it needs the remedy that is found only in Jesus. Learning how to tell the story in such a way that does not let sin off the hook but also is gentle and respectful—that takes time and is rooted in the promises of Jesus. Your goal is not to make others upset, although realizing their sin may do that. Your goal is to share the whole story, the reality of sin along with the hope of the Savior.

Look at the differences between how Jesus addressed outsiders and insiders. To those outside the faith, He spoke truth but leaned heavily on grace. Never did He sugarcoat their situation, but He also didn't act as if they were the scum of the earth.

He did not treat them as enemies; He treated them as people. Now, how did He talk to the insiders, the scribes and the Pharisees, the ones who knew God's Word and should have known better? With them, He brought a strong word of God's truth and Law. Still full of grace and the Gospel, but He did not let them off the hook for what they had become and what their actions had created. Let us follow this example as well, seeking to find a balance between truth and grace, Law and Gospel.

Let your storytelling be personal. You are not the hero, but that does not mean you are not a part of the story. You are the messenger sharing the story of the King. You are the best kind of messenger: one who is a witness to the great works of Jesus. Learn how to share what Jesus is doing in your life. This comes only through experience. You can't just sit back and think about this. Share with your Christian friends to gain experience, but learn how to talk about the work of Jesus in your life. Talk about the grace you receive on a daily basis. Tell the story of how you are learning about constant repentance and the deep well of love God has for you. Seek to see it in your daily life so you can learn how to share it with others. Allow them to see that you struggle with sin. Our story is not about being sinless; it is about a Savior who has come to redeem. Make Him the hero. Share how good He is.

Your story is a gift God has given you to bring His Good News to the disconnected. Learning how to share it in a way that is relatable but does not change the message is part of your discipleship journey. The goal should never be to simply try to prove others wrong into belief, to shout them down until they are broken. Instead, defend your hope, share your hope, with gentleness and respect. Share the story of Jesus in your life and His mighty work in this world.

Those Inside

> And I heard a loud voice in heaven, saying, "Now the salvation and the power and the kingdom of our God and the authority of His Christ have come, for the accuser of our brothers has been thrown down, who accuses them day and night before our God. And they have conquered him by the blood of the Lamb and by the word of their testimony, for they loved not their lives even unto death." (Revelation 12:10–11)

There are few things as good as sitting around a fire sharing life with friends and family. As technology both brings us together and pulls us farther apart, time spent person to person without a screen is uplifting. For Christians, this time also takes on another aspect. There is a weariness to this life. The burden of following Jesus is light, but the enemy will work to make it feel as if it weighs many tons. Another gift given to the Body of Christ is sharing how Jesus is at work in their lives.

Look at the above verses from Revelation. There are two ways that one fights in the battles of spiritual warfare against the accuser. First is by the blood of the Lamb. Jesus' blood is and always will be the chief defeat of our enemy. This is a work we cannot do. How, then, do we join in the fight with "the word of [our] testimony"? Telling the story of Jesus at work in our lives is the battle we can fight. Through these stories, the eyewitness testimony, we confess not only who Jesus is but also how He is at work. That emboldens the brothers and sisters in Christ. It encourages the Body. We should all be asking one another, "What is Jesus doing in your life? Where have you needed His grace? To what good works is He calling you?"

Kingdom people, Christians, disciples, have a story to tell. Yet often our gaze is drawn elsewhere. We fall in love with the shiny things of this world instead of the things of Jesus. Coming together to share our stories encourages one another and fights the battle of spiritual warfare, but it also reminds us how quickly we can be led astray. The path of discipleship is meant to be a journey together, but it doesn't need to be traveled in silence. The journey includes laughter and the joy of hearing the good works of Jesus. We mourn together along the way. Stories of praise, thanksgiving, and lament should be shared by all. It is a blessing to share in this journey together, and telling the story of Jesus helps us to follow Him.

Do not neglect this within the Body of Christ. As with most things, humans will seek to try to run to one end of an idea or the other. Reaction is preferred to tension. But here let there be tension. Sharing the story of Jesus with unbelievers is important. Bringing those stories to your communities of faith is edifying. Do not get sucked into living in only one world or the other. The benefit of following Jesus is that you can and should do both. His story is not reserved only for the lost, and it is not exclusive to the found. His story is freely told in all venues.

Sometimes, sharing the story of Jesus within the Body of Christ will lead to conviction, and that is good. We are tempted to wander astray. But sharing who Jesus is with one another will shed light on areas in our lives where we have turned a blind eye to sin. This is a difficult but important part of our journey. We are called to point people back to Jesus, to follow Him. When we see fellow Christians wandering off the path, we share the story of Jesus to bring them back to His ways. Conviction is not an evil thing; it is a gift that reminds us of the grace of Jesus, that even as we wander, He is the one who took the cross for us.

LEAVE SHAME AT THE DOOR

> For I am not ashamed of the gospel, for it is the power of God for salvation to everyone who believes, to the Jew first and also to the Greek. (Romans 1:16)

Our enemy is working overtime to make us feel shame in sharing our story. He wants us to feel unprepared, foolish, and unqualified. His number one goal is to shake the foundations of the people of God.

Being unprepared is an opening for the enemy to work his way into our hearts. Learn to differentiate between *being* unprepared and *feeling* unprepared. Being unprepared is something you can work on. Make a plan to grow, and return to the question "What is my next step?" Do it in increments. Be in the Word, look for resources, and find mentors in the faith who can help you. You can work to be prepared and see the Holy Spirit at work through your actions. However, if you are *feeling* unprepared, even though you have put in the time and effort, that is the enemy working to keep you from sharing the story. That can be solved only through prayer. Seek the Lord on it. Trust His promises. He is the one who works through you. You can overcome only by the blood of the Lamb and the word of testimony.

Looking or feeling foolish is another tactic the enemy will use to keep you from sharing Jesus' story. This is reflected once again with the idea of wanting to share Jesus but not look weird. No one wants to look foolish in front of their friends. But look at the words from Romans above. Do not be ashamed of the Gospel; it is the power of God for salvation. Trust that when you tell Jesus' story, as you follow Him, He will work in that situation. In your sharing and storytelling, He is at work. Trust Him. Run away from the lies that you will look foolish. Understand that there are people who will hear you, whose hearts the Holy Spirit has prepared. There will be people who do not hear you; then you move forward. Do not treat them as lesser, but know that it is God who changes hearts, not you. You are the messenger. Don't ever stop bringing the message.

Often people feel unqualified to be storytellers of the Kingdom. They look at their lives and say, "You don't know what I have done, what sins I have committed." That may be true. But let's look at some of the people God used throughout Scripture:

- Abraham tried to pass his wife off as his sister so other men could have sex with her because he was a coward.

- Moses was a murderer.

- David was an adulterer and murderer.

- Rahab was a prostitute.

- Peter denied knowing Jesus three times.

- Thomas doubted.

- Before he was Paul, Saul persecuted Christians, standing by while Stephen was stoned to death.

These people appear to be unqualified. But God used them anyway. Sinful people have always carried the message of God. That is a fact. You are not different. Jesus has redeemed you—that is your qualification. God uses His saints, His people who have been washed clean in the blood of the Lamb. He has always done this, and He will continue to do it. You are not unqualified. Jesus walks with you.

As you tell this story, you are never alone. The Holy Spirit is in you. Jesus walks with you. The Father watches over you. The Body of Christ surrounds you. Never think that you are alone in this endeavor. There will be many opportunities to share your story, both with those outside of faith and with those inside the Body. This is the best story you could ever tell.

The Story for You

As a storyteller, make sure to remember that this story is for you as well. Following Jesus into the world does not guarantee safety. Rather, it is a calling to step out of your front door as a messenger of the King. It will not always be safe, but it will be good. As you learn to tell the story, remember, it is for you.

The promised Messiah is for you. In Genesis 3, when God first made the promise that the Offspring of man would crush the head of the serpent, God was thinking about you. He was looking forward to the day when you would be a part of His kingdom. When the world fell apart and sin began its ugly invasion, God knew that one day you would be a part of it. He could not stand idly by and let you suffer. Instead, He prepared a response: a Messiah, His Son. All of this for you.

The cross is for you. It may be foolishness and a stumbling block to others, but to those who believe, it is the saving grace. Christ crucified is the declaration of people who know they can do nothing, that their Savior took their place and in Him they have found redemption, hope, and peace. This is your story. Christ crucified for you.

The Kingdom is for you. God declares that there will one day be a new heaven and a new earth. Creation will be restored to what it was supposed to be before the fall. Everything will be made new. There will be no more suffering, no more crying, no more sin. Death will be destroyed. The Body of Christ, His Church, will live resurrected in the perfect glory of this new creation. Every act will be one of worship. While we wait, Jesus is not withholding this Kingdom to come. No, He asks us to be its messengers. He sends us out as His hands and feet. Through our actions, we bring small glimpses of His kingdom into the world. Empowered by the Gospel, we seek to do the good works that are set for us. It is our confession as we follow our King, what we can do as a small light of that Kingdom in this dark world.

The story is for you. Go and tell it. Earn your voice with friends, neighbors, and co-workers and tell this magnificent story of the King who would die for His people. Share how it is at work in your life. Speak to the reality of this living story that brings with it hope and peace. Of a God who would not abandon His creation. Of the Son who would sacrifice everything to save it. This story is yours to tell. You have been sent out with it; do not keep it to yourself.

Learn to become a better storyteller. Begin by sharing with your Christian brothers and sisters. In them, you will find an eager audience to hear the work of Jesus in your life. Ask questions and seek out mentors who can guide you in how to tell the story. Not only that, but hearing their stories of following Jesus will also bless you. Mentors, share those stories! Seek others who need to hear and imitate your life as you seek to imitate Christ. The Body of Christ is a space of encouragement and growth where you can hone your craft and learn to tell the story better and better.

This will not be the capstone of the discipleship journey, but it is one that pushes you into new realms. Following Jesus means living in your vocations. It means loving God and others through your actions. It means caring for the poor, helping those in need, and serving through all manner of ways. All those things give glimpses of the Kingdom. How do people find Jesus in their lives? "So faith comes from hearing, and hearing through the word of Christ" (Romans 10:17). You cannot simply let your actions do the talking. God works through everyday means. Just as He created the universe through the Word, He has chosen to use your words to facilitate the creation of belief. Sharing this story is an everyday way in which God works through you, a member of His kingdom.

You may feel overwhelmed by fear. Remember, "there is no fear in love, but perfect love casts out fear" (1 John 4:18). The love of Jesus compels us to tell His story. As we do, we learn how best to tell it and whom to tell it to. But it doesn't rest all on your shoulders. Seek to be an instrument of the Holy Spirit. Find Jesus in the places He has prepared for you. Tell His story.

OPEN WITH PRAYER

Ask for a volunteer to open with prayer. Rotate who does this each time you get together. Praying in front of people may scare you, but it is worth growing in the practice. Praying together is part of what the Body of Christ does. Not only is it our connection to God but it also gives an example of how we live on this discipleship journey.

FROM LAST TIME

How's your next step going?

DISCUSSION

1. What jumped out to you in this chapter?

2. What is your favorite memory of seeing a movie as a kid?

3. What did you learn about telling the story of Jesus?

DO IT

Write your Jesus story. How does His story interact with yours?

THE THREE QUESTIONS

Read through 1 Peter 3:14–16. Answer the three questions. Be prepared to share with the group.

1. What is God saying?

2. What is He calling me to do?

3. What is my next step?

CLOSING

Make sure you know when you are getting together next.

Pray for one another. Take prayer requests and close in prayer. Spread out the prayer requests so as many people are praying as are available.

BEFORE NEXT TIME

Read the "Simple" devotion and chapter 11, answer the questions for that chapter, and prepare to share how your next step for 1 Peter 3:14–16 is going!

Simple

My son, do not forget my teaching, but let your heart keep my commandments, for length of days and years of life and peace they will add to you. Let not steadfast love and faithfulness forsake you; bind them around your neck; write them on the tablet of your heart. So you will find favor and good success in the sight of God and man. Trust in the Lord with all your heart, and do not lean on your own understanding. In all your ways acknowledge Him, and He will make straight your paths. Be not wise in your own eyes; fear the Lord, and turn away from evil.

Proverbs 3:1–7

What do you do to teach a child to ride a bike? Maybe at a young age you start the child off on a tricycle—something that won't tip no matter what, something low to the ground and solid. There is little chance of injury. Then the next step might be a balance bike. No pedals, just two wheels and feet on the ground. After that comes the big kid's bike with training wheels. Once you've got the child riding on the training wheels for a while, you start teaching how to ride without the training wheels. The child will fall over, but after practice will be able to ride circles in the driveway and then start to ride out with friends. Riding will become second nature and muscle memory. Instead of focusing on how to ride, the child will get to just enjoy the ride.

That is how this book functions with discipleship. It has given you some tools to help you see, discuss, and experience the journey. As you grow in using these tools, you might find yourself doing them naturally. Good. They are training wheels. They are here to help you, but the goal is not that the tools become the method. The goal is that you are a person who continually trusts the promises of Jesus and seeks to follow Him.

Moment to moment, you are a person living that life. Trusting, seeking, and following. These final two chapters will dive into lifelong discipleship and how it is part of your identity.

What has been the most beneficial chapter for you so far? What do you think is the greatest thing you have learned? Write a list of some people who you think might benefit from walking through this book. Pray that you might be the person to lead them through it.

Share this with your group. Take time together to dive into these questions. In the final two chapters, you might find some conviction. Work through that. Ask the Lord what He might be speaking to you and how the Holy Spirit is at work in your life.

> Lord, every day let Your promises be the
> anchor for who I am. As those truths work
> in my life, give me a heart that seeks after
> You. Make my path straight and bless me as I
> follow You. Amen.

Discipleship in Life

Imagine your number one vacation destination. Maybe it is a cabin tucked away in the mountains. You might be the type of person looking to enjoy a bustling metropolis and see the sights. Whatever this place is, you have done the research. If there is a book or travel blog concerning this locale, you have read it. You've spent time online researching the best places to stay, the sights to see, and the thriftiest ways of getting there. With nervous and excited jitters, you pack your bags, set your alarm clock, and try to find some way to fall asleep. You're going the next day—how could you possibly sleep! Your alarm breaks through your restless sleep. You wipe your eyes, get up, get ready. Today is the day. You grab your bag, do a quick mental check of your things . . . run back to your bedside table to grab the phone charger you almost forgot, and hurriedly toss it in your bag. With a spring in your step, you grab your things to head out. But then you remember what security could be like at the airport. What if something were to go wrong on your flight? That could really mess things up. Who knows what this place you have been researching for the past several years could actually be like? As everything starts getting in your head, you decide may it would just be better to sit on the couch. Grabbing the closest snack and changing back into your pajamas, you plop down and watch a Netflix documentary on the place you wanted to go. Isn't this safer anyway?

Imagine if that actually happened. It seems far-fetched. But isn't that how we often treat being members of the kingdom of God? We put in the research, are convinced of where we are being led, and then promptly find a distraction. Because it is much safer that way, much more comfortable. And comfort is one of the gods of culture that we don't want to give up. You read through this book and then just let the ideas sit on the shelf. Again, this is not some holy or one true way to grow as a disciple. But it does not allow for you to simply read and sit still. This is not meant to be solely a discussion guide where you sit around talking about how you might be able to apply what you have learned. No. Waiting in front of you is the world where discipleship is put into practice. Head, heart, and hands. Growing in the ways of Jesus. Fear of failure, seeking comfort, and our own human ideas distract us from taking this journey into our everyday lives.

Failure

What happens when you fail? At some point, this life of discipleship will seem like too much effort, the old sinful self will come calling, and you will heed its enticing and elusive call. Lies whispered in your ear tell you that once you struggle or fail, then it is done; God is seeking only those who will be perfect. You may set up levels of Christians in your mind. There are those who are successful and follow, those who just show up, and those who confess with their mouth but turn away.

All of us end up handling the fear of failure differently. For some, it is motivation to simply put their nose to the grindstone and work. While self-discipline and a good work ethic are to be admired, when the driving force is the dread of defeat, it leads not to fruitfulness but instead to exhaustion. There is a difference between being tired from working hard and driving yourself into the ground with weariness. The former is a joy, hitting the bed at the end of the day knowing you spent your time well. The other leads to sleepless nights, tossing and turning filled with worry and anxiety.

Others, when encountering the thoughts of failure, freeze up. Instead of following Jesus, all they can see is how such an endeavor might go wrong. "What if"s fill their brain, and instead of walking in the power of the promise, they simply do nothing. It becomes a protective shell in which they try to hide. The problem? When one does nothing, it quickly shows. Unlike those who may work harder to stave off failure, who produce fruit that may look good but actually causes them harm, those who freeze fail to produce. They, too, end up drained because all they see is how it could all fall apart.

What is the answer to failure? Return to your source of power. Remember these words from Scripture:

> Cast your burden on the LORD, and He will sustain you; He will never permit the righteous to be moved. (Psalm 55:22)

> Therefore I tell you, do not be anxious about your life, what you will eat or what you will drink, nor about your body, what you will put on. Is not life more than food, and the body more than clothing?

... But seek first the kingdom of God and His righteousness, and all these things will be added to you. Therefore do not be anxious about tomorrow, for tomorrow will be anxious for itself. Sufficient for the day is its own trouble. (Matthew 6:25, 33–34)

Come to Me, all who labor and are heavy laden, and I will give you rest. Take My yoke upon you, and learn from Me, for I am gentle and lowly in heart, and you will find rest for your souls. For My yoke is easy, and My burden is light. (Matthew 11:28–30)

Do not be anxious about anything, but in everything by prayer and supplication with thanksgiving let your requests be made known to God. And the peace of God, which surpasses all understanding, will guard your hearts and your minds in Christ Jesus. (Philippians 4:6–7)

Humble yourselves, therefore, under the mighty hand of God so that at the proper time He may exalt you, casting all your anxieties on Him, because He cares for you. (1 Peter 5:6–7)

The answer to failure is trust. We trust that even when we step out of our doors and mess up, God is good; His burdens are light. When we recognize a weariness coming from a fear of failure, we return to His promises. We trust that when we are not experiencing the light burdens and peace that Jesus promises, then we should return to Him. Too often we seek an answer to our fear of walking as a disciple by asking what we should do. Instead, ask, "Lord, show me what You have done." Because one thing is for sure: you will fail. There will be days when it all goes off the tracks. Sometimes those days turn into longer stretches. But the remedy is still the same: return to the promises of Jesus.

It has taken me years to identify and realize that when I fear failure, I am a person who freezes. For a long time, I think I had hoped that it wasn't the case and it might be something I grew out of from my youth. But now I think it might be something that I see as a warning sign, rather than something I need to get rid of. It is like a tornado siren letting me know what is coming. Instead of trying to remove the fear on my own, I have learned to use it to quickly identify what is happening in me, to show me that I have wandered far from the source and am trying, once again, to accomplish the work of the Kingdom on my own.

Once again, confession is an incredible tool. If you wish to battle against your fear of failure, to return to trusting the promises of Jesus, confess your fear and anxiety. As I learned about my own reaction to fear of failure, I have slowly built up relationships with a few people I trust whom I turn to in these times. I go to these fellow brothers and sisters in Christ and confess this fear, the things that are freezing me and keeping me from following Jesus. It still hasn't quite become second nature, but I have seen growth. Why? Because when I confess this sin to them, they bring me back to the foot of the cross. I am learning that I can trust Scripture when it says, "Therefore, confess your sins to one another and pray for one another, that you may be healed. The prayer of a righteous person has great power as it is working" (James 5:16). It brings me back to the source, to the promise.

Now, what about pure failure? Not fear, but those times when you actually fail? Maybe it is because of sinful desire or maybe because you just messed it up. Confession. Return again to the promise. Let that confession lead you to repentance. Not only to God but also to those you may have hurt along the way. The journey of discipleship is not without its failures; it's how we handle the failures that matters. Will you ignore them and simply try to hide your sin, putting on the mask of perfection and self-righteousness? Or will you throw caution to the wind and live in licentiousness, sinning just because you can? No. The answer is a life filled with repentance. Confession and absolution are vital gifts. Return to Jesus. Seek His forgiveness. When you run far and think that there isn't enough grace left for you, remember your Baptism. Partake in the Lord's Supper. These are gifts for you not because you are perfect but because God knew that you would fail and feel unworthy. Through His Son, He has made you worthy. Through His Sacraments, He brings you that worthiness many times over.

Comfort

Comfort is a chief idol of American Christians. Look at all the things we have given away in our pursuit of comfort—caring for the poor, sick, and orphan, ceding our responsibilities to governments and secular organizations. The church in the United States has become more about showmanship than discipleship. Whether called by the bells ringing from the steeples of our stone edifices or the wail of the electric guitars from our worship centers, American Christians want to show up for an hour on Sunday, experience God through their preferred means, and then go home. We used to build hospitals, orphanages, and food pantries. Now we build youth rooms, gyms, and larger steeples. We think if we can only provide or be provided with what we want for our religious consumption, then we will be okay. Cordoning ourselves off, we have become gluttons of faith, saying that we want to be challenged yet all the while kicking and screaming when anyone would dare make us feel uncomfortable—including God.

We have become a church based not on being comforted but on being comfortable.

This same idol of comfort expresses itself in the journey of discipleship. We find excuses not to seek or follow Jesus. We would rather be comfortable. We find reasons not to love God or our neighbor because that might require us to change our lives and schedules. Looking at the week, we assign God the times He can and cannot have. Discipleship is part of what we do around people from our church but not in our everyday lives. Our pet sins sit in a safe place where we tell God it is okay and He doesn't need to be worried about those things. They're not that big of a deal. Seeking comfort allows us to live in an insular echo chamber where nothing disturbs us.

Seeking God will shake us out of our comfort. The Holy Spirit will work conviction in our hearts. He will shake us out of our malaise to see where we have elevated convenience above the calling of being Kingdom people. Vocation reminds us that as we follow Jesus, He has us where He needs us. Instead of being comfortable, we seek to step out into the world as His messengers. As we do this, we find that being comforted is much more rewarding than being comfortable. Look at how the Scriptures talk about comfort:

> Even though I walk through the valley of the shadow of death, I will fear no evil, for You are with me; Your rod and Your staff, they comfort me. (Psalm 23:4)

> Remember Your word to Your servant, in which You have made me hope. This is my comfort in my affliction, that Your promise gives me life. (Psalm 119:49–50)

> Seeing the crowds, He went up on the mountain, and when He sat down, His disciples came to Him. And He opened His mouth and taught them, saying: "Blessed are the poor in spirit, for theirs is the kingdom of heaven. Blessed are those who mourn, for they shall be comforted. Blessed are the meek, for they shall inherit the earth. Blessed are those who hunger and thirst for righteousness, for they shall be satisfied. Blessed are the merciful, for they shall receive mercy. Blessed are the pure in heart, for they shall see God. Blessed are the peacemakers, for they shall be called sons of God. Blessed are those who are persecuted for righteousness' sake, for theirs is the kingdom of heaven. Blessed are you when others revile you and persecute you and utter all kinds of evil against you falsely on My account. Rejoice and be glad, for your reward is great in heaven, for so they persecuted the prophets who were before you." (Matthew 5:1–12)

God comforts those who are living in the world, not those seeking to be comfortable outside of it. This does not mean we do not rest. But it also means that we do not seek after our own comfort. We don't make excuses not to seek after God. Instead, we look and are honest, and we admit our own selfish desire when it creeps up on us. We live in the midst of community so that trusted brothers and sisters in Christ can call us out of our comfort and into following Jesus. It means that we do not excuse ourselves. We may have boundaries and know our limits, but we don't seek our own convenience over being messengers of the Kingdom in our words and our actions.

Fighting against our own comfort and convenience will be hard. There are few people who enjoy discomfort. Instead, we understand that discomfort is a way through. It is what happens when we are growing and learning. If the life of a disciple is one of continued re-creation, then it will often be uncomfortable. Through the process of sanctification, Jesus is making us back into what we were originally created to be. Our natural state is to live in our sinful nature. The process of discipleship shows us that the ways of Jesus are not only better but are actually how we were created to be. It rips apart our comfort. Loving God and loving our neighbors is a concept that is built up by Jesus.

Stepping out of our convenience is simple. Just keep asking the Lord, "What? Lord, what do You need me to do where You have placed me? What is my next step?" Take a tough look at your life and ask where you are seeking comfort over calling. What areas of your vocations are you pushing to the side? Go to the Lord in prayer. Ask that He take down this idol so that you may follow Him.

Seek to be comforted in the midst of your vocation, not to be comfortable at your convenience.

Our Own Ideas

As we daily follow Jesus, our own feelings of worthiness and accomplishment can get in the way. Your worthiness is not measured by you. It is measured by what Jesus has done. "I will greatly rejoice in the LORD; my soul shall exult in my God, for He has clothed me with the garments of salvation; He has covered me with the robe of righteousness, as a bridegroom decks himself like a priest with a beautiful headdress, and as a bride adorns herself with her jewels" (Isaiah 61:10). You are covered in the garments of salvation. You don't have to be some super Christian to be living your life as an everyday disciple. Lean into those promises again.

How we see our accomplishments as disciples can greatly affect our daily journey. There are many times when we are trying to move ahead, to just keep following Jesus. If you were to hike the Lost Mine Trail in Big Bend National Park, you would find some incredible views. But what you would also find is a false summit. Halfway up the trail, mountain forest opens up into a beautiful view of a magnificent valley. But this is not the end of the trail. It may seem like the end, but it is the middle. From there, you hike the second half of the trail—a series of steep switchbacks. Rocks litter the path, and all you can do is look at your feet and wonder if you were a fool to not just appreciate the view of the valley and head back to the car. You hope each switchback you encounter is the final one. But no, you just continue up, keeping your face down to make sure you don't trip and fall over a stone jutting out from the ground. Finally, you cross between two boulders and come to the flat top of a mountain. The valley view pales in comparison to this. The Chisos Mountains spread out in front of you, daggering their way across Texas and into Mexico. You can see for miles, and your breath catches. Taking a moment, you look back to see how far you have come. The switchbacks and steep trails—which felt like torture and as if you were barely able to keep upright, much less move forward—have brought you to this vista. After taking it in and celebrating at the top with a snack, you start the trek back down into the valley to your car waiting at the trailhead.

This is how discipleship works. There will be days when all you can do is see the short steps ahead of you, and you just put one foot in front of the other. Even when you reach a goal or turn a corner, you find another steep incline ahead of you. But as you journey, you will find moments on the mountaintop—those beautiful vistas that make you catch your breath. The amazing ways in which God has been moving, at one point hidden, have now become clear. It is hard work, but it is simple. Put one foot in front of the other. Start each day planning to follow Jesus by just taking one more step.

But take moments to view how far you have come too. Keep a journal or notes to see your discipleship journey. This is not to build up your pride, but instead to see that as you have followed Jesus, He has kept His promises! Don't wait for the mountaintops to take a moment, catch your breath, rest, and see how far the Lord has brought you! As you journey, it is good to rest and see the Holy Spirit's work in your life, to recognize that there is joy in the journey.

Finally, don't forget that it is not all mountaintops. It is easy to get discouraged if every day all you are waiting for is the spiritual high. Even Jesus didn't stay on the mountaintop. At the Transfiguration—one of the greatest spiritual mountaintop experiences of all time—Jesus knew that He had to leave the mountain to continue His ministry, even though the disciples begged to build tents and stay. But Jesus had to leave the mountain to go to the cross. We cannot live our lives on the mountaintop either. It's unattainable for us. We would constantly be looking for the next spiritual high, the next thing that would beat the last one. Instead, we follow the trail where it leads, up to the mountaintops and back into the valleys. Jesus is just as much the King of the valleys as He is of the mountaintops.

A disciple is a person who trusts the promises of Jesus and seeks to follow Him. Trusting. Seeking. Following. Three simple concepts lived out in the daily life of a disciple. Constantly at work, the Holy Spirit is using these means to transform your life. Your salvation is not a trophy that you set on a shelf and dust off a couple of times a month. It is a tool to be used as you go about your day. It is both promise and power.

Living life daily as a disciple is living simply. Trusting, seeking, and following. Living in that rhythm over and over again. It is able to be done by the church worker and the college student. There is no limit or bar for the person to walk in these ways, to be on this journey. Our world is constantly trying to classify people and put them in categories. This is not something that is absent from the realm of faith. In our sinful nature, we set up hierarchies of the faithful, as if some are greater than others, more worthy of being followers of Jesus. But that is not how discipleship works. Jesus spent time with both the Pharisees and the tax collectors, the scribes and the lepers. The twelve disciples were made up of all kinds of tradesmen. It is not a complicated process. It is simple so all people can follow it.

Life in Rhythm

As you live out this discipleship journey, you will learn that it is a rhythm. You trust the promises of Jesus, which leads you deeper into seeking after Him. As you seek Him and learn more about who He is, you are called to follow Him wherever He has placed you. Then as you follow, you realize you need to trust Him more, which leads back to seeking, then back again to following Him.

These are parts of a whole. Trusting the promises of Jesus is where you find His power in your life. Salvation is proclaimed again and again. As you seek after Him, the Word of God settles into your heart and the Holy Spirit works. As that work happens, you are led into your world, following Jesus. Trusting Jesus is foundational. It cannot be changed. It is the bedrock. But being a disciple is about all three: trusting, which leads to seeking and following. That is where it will always lead.

As you learn that rhythm, remember that each disciple is at his or her own part of the journey. Don't judge others because they haven't come as far as you have. Don't be disappointed that you are not as far along as others. This is the Body of Christ at work.

Check in where you are. Keep in mind that there will always be temptation to run in one direction or another. We are often tempted to lean too deeply into seeking or following, which can result in putting trusting Jesus on the back burner.

Putting a higher emphasis on seeking leads to a knowledge that puffs up. Here, it's easy to place all attention on knowing the right things. Be it Scripture, doctrine, or dogma, if you only know enough and correctly, then you can be a true disciple. Knowing the Bible and theology is a good thing. But if it is done to the neglect of application, then it is just knowledge for knowledge's sake. This can lead to a form of Law-based faith that only allows for right knowledge to be the entryway for discipleship. Unchecked, it will give lip service to the promises of Jesus, putting the onus of salvation on knowledge instead. Even if those words aren't said, the reality can be seen in actions and arguments.

Similarly, if following Jesus into the world is not connected to seeking Him, it will lead off the path. When following is overemphasized, discipleship is gauged by good works. Only if you are doing the right things can you possibly be a disciple. It doesn't matter what God has said; it just matters what you do. This will often push love to the realm of tolerance. Sin is cast aside, and Jesus is good only for His social, moral, and ethical teachings. Following is less about seeing where Jesus has placed you in your life and more about the rat race of trying to do enough good things to be considered a good person. There is no room for opposition because that sends the message that you do not love people. This pushes seeking out of the way and untethers you from trusting the promises of Jesus.

The promises of Jesus are the anchor. Grounding how we seek and follow, they must remain at center. The weight of those promises draws together seeking and following so that they are not at war with each other but instead are interwoven parts of the whole. Trusting Jesus will lead us to seek Him. Seeking Him will show us places in our lives where we need to follow Him. As we seek and follow, we return to the promises because we need the Gospel for us.

Growing in this comes through experience as you walk in the ways of Jesus in your everyday life. Some things will come easy; others will be more difficult. But that doesn't stop you. Discipleship is about continuing forward. Let those promises propel you into seeking Jesus more in the Bible. Learn how to hear God through His Word. Experience how that affects your life. Follow Jesus wherever He may lead. Watch how it affects your relationships and the world around you. Seek the Kingdom wherever you are.

When and where are good times to dig into discipleship? Wherever you are going. Discipleship happens in worship, during Bible studies, in homes, on ball fields, on hikes, and on shopping trips. As you are going, invite others on the journey with you. The Christian life is not contained to the four walls of the church. Within those buildings, be they adorned with stained glass or the cafeteria of a local school, God meets His people to send them into the world. In fact, He has already gone ahead of us. Do not confine the discipleship journey to what happens while you are at church functions. Those times are meant to build us up for the work that God has for us to do in the world, not to contain His work to a specific place.

Jesus is sending you as salt and light into the world. Cherish the time you spend with the Body of Christ in worship, study, and fellowship. Invest time in seeking God throughout the week. As you go about your daily tasks, carve time out to abide in Him. Write down how you see Him moving in your world. Take that back to the Word and see how God is speaking. Take it back to the Body of Christ to hear their thoughts and to be blessed by your testimony.

Be bold! Follow Jesus in every place you go. Let your vocations be all about loving God and loving your neighbors. Pray for everyone around you. The barista at your coffee shop? Ask how you can pray for her. The high schooler scanning your items at the grocery store? Ask him if there is something that you can pray for him about. The family you see at the park, your mechanic, your next-door neighbor, the waiter at the restaurant? Pray for them all. Watch how God works in changing your heart as you pray for all of the people around you. Ask them for prayer requests; show them that you care. As you see needs around you, don't ask permission—find ways to serve people. Jesus has sent you! You don't have to ask your pastor if you can serve someone; just do it! The kingdom of God is at hand. He is giving the world glimpses of that Kingdom through you. Tell the story of the Kingdom wherever you go through your actions and through your words.

Discipleship doesn't happen in a vacuum. It happens in the real places of your life. The Creator of the universe, who sent His Son as a sacrifice for you, invites you to get to know Him better and to live as one of the people of His kingdom. Discipleship is about the promises of Jesus, which give you salvation and strength. The Bible is not just a nice book that sits on your nightstand. It is the real Word of God given to you to hear who

He is and what He is calling you to do, not in some weird, theoretical way, but on Monday. He is inviting you to follow Him, as a Kingdom person, a member of the family, a friend. You don't have to ask where that is supposed to be. You just have to walk outside.

OPEN WITH PRAYER

Ask for a volunteer to open with prayer. Rotate who does this each time you get together. Praying in front of people may scare you, but it is worth growing in the practice. Praying together is part of what the Body of Christ does. Not only is it our connection to God but it also gives an example of how we live on this discipleship journey.

FROM LAST TIME

How's your next step going?

DISCUSSION

1. What jumped out to you in this chapter?

2. What is your reaction to fear of failure? Do you lean in and overwork? Or do you freeze up and do nothing?

3. How has God used failure to teach you something in the past? How have you seen His grace in the midst of it?

4. In what areas of your life do you seek comfort and convenience over Jesus?

5. How can you be bold in your discipleship this week?

THE THREE QUESTIONS

Read through Ephesians 2:8–10, answer the three questions, and be prepared to share with the group.

1. What is God saying?

2. What is He calling me to do?

3. What is my next step?

CLOSING

Make sure you know when you are getting together next.

Pray for one another. Take prayer requests and close in prayer. Spread out the prayer requests so as many people are praying as are available.

BEFORE NEXT TIME

Read chapter 12, answer the questions for that chapter, and be ready to share how your next step for Ephesians 2:8–10 is going!

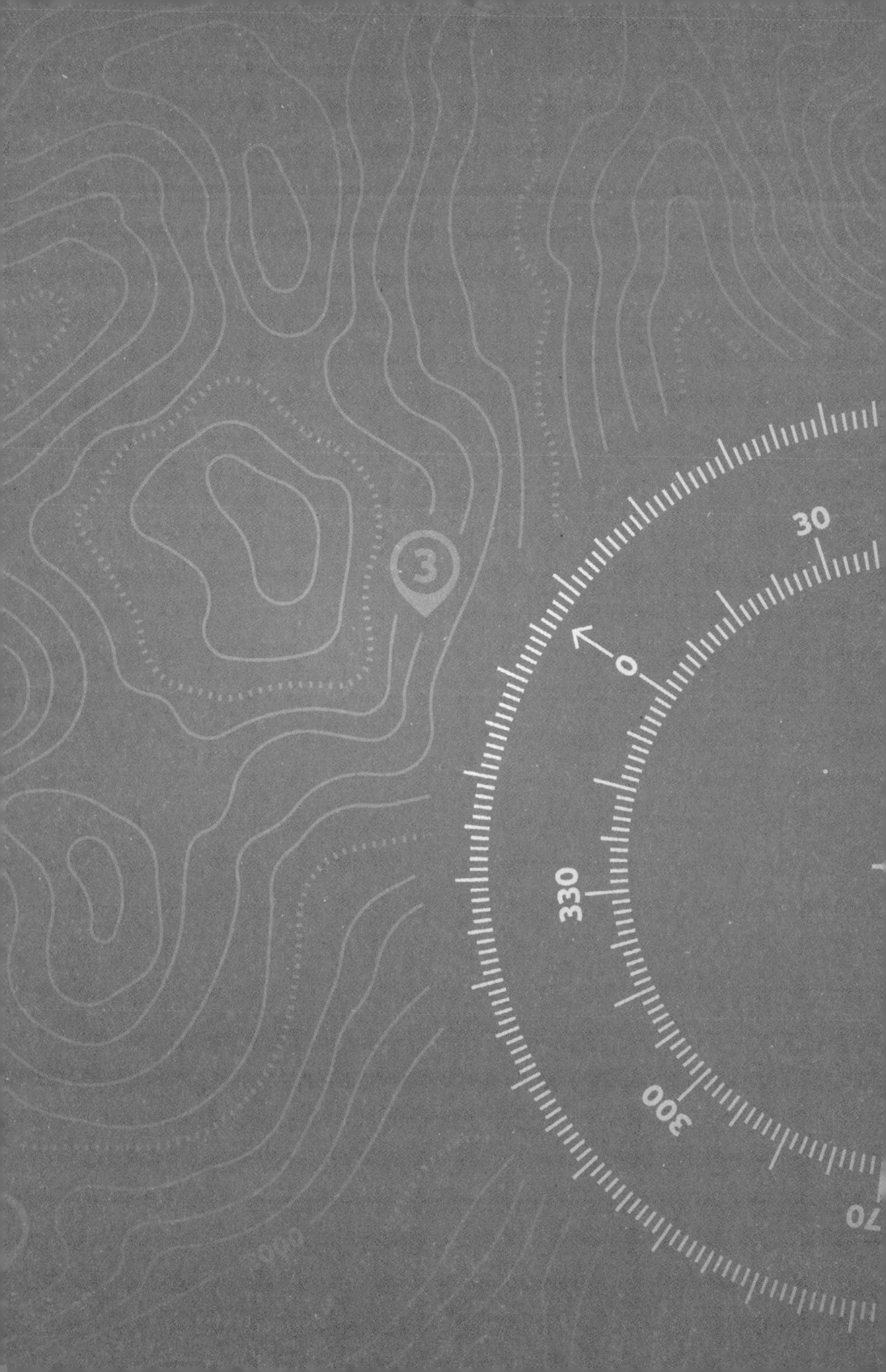
3
30
0
330
300

Identity

This world needs more Kingdom messengers. More Christians. More disciples. It needs you. Why? Because it needs Jesus, and you are a person chosen to carry His message into the world. At your Baptism, you were saved from sin, but you were also brought into a family that has a calling. That's how God works. He does not stop giving to His people. Salvation is not a stepping-stone into a different life. It *is* new life. That new life changes who we are to the core. Our identity is transformed as those waters flow over us. Baptism realigns who we are. It brings us into Jesus; we are buried in Him. There is no longer any piece of us that is not covered by His blood. Baptismal identity transforms who we are.

An interesting thing about this transformation: it affects more than just our salvation. When we were purchased at the cross by Jesus' sacrifice, a shift began in who we are. Foundationally, our lives changed. Whether we were baptized as an infant or at a time in our life that we can remember, we were changed by Baptism. Why? Because there is nothing in our lives that God doesn't seek to redeem. After the fall, not only was our connection with God severed but everything in the world also became touched by sin. God did not create the world to exist in a state of heartache where war, pestilence, and strife would cause the soul to break down. These are all symptoms of sin in a world that is a shadow of what it was meant to be. Sin shifted creation to the point that even it looks for the coming day when Jesus will return:

> For I consider that the sufferings of this present time are not worth comparing with the glory that is to be revealed to us. For the creation waits with eager longing for the revealing of the sons of God. For the creation was subjected to futility, not willingly, but because of Him who subjected it, in hope that the creation itself will be set free from its bondage to corruption and obtain the freedom of the glory of the children of God. For we know that the whole creation has been groaning together in the pains of childbirth until now. And not only the creation, but we ourselves, who have the firstfruits of the Spirit, groan inwardly as we wait eagerly for adoption as sons, the redemption of our bodies. (Romans 8:18–23)

God's whole creation has been eagerly awaiting you. It has been groaning in expectation. Why? Because you are a messenger of the Kingdom. You are called to declare the marvelous story of the one who is to come. Even God's creation calls out, hoping to see the days of the sons and daughters of the family of God. This signals that the Messiah has come, that creation, too, will one day be restored. Redemption is not just about fire insurance, a get-out-of-hell-free card. Being purchased by the blood of the Lamb is entrance into a new identity. You are no longer what you do or what you did. No longer do you need to be defined by accomplishments or accolades, by wrongdoing or brokenness. As the baptismal waters passed over, they washed away the old identity that grasped to drag you down and away from your inheritance. In that simple water combined with the Word of God, the almighty hand of the Creator reached down and claimed you. Your identity no longer belongs to the fallen ways. No. You are a child of God. There was nothing you could do, so God did it all and sent His Son for you.

> Do you not know that all of us who have been baptized into Christ Jesus were baptized into His death? We were buried therefore with Him by baptism into death, in order that, just as Christ was raised from the dead by the glory of the Father, we too might walk in newness of life. For if we have been united with Him in a death like His, we shall certainly be united with Him in a resurrection like His. We know that our old self was crucified with Him in order that the body of sin might be brought to nothing, so that we would no longer be enslaved to sin. For one who has died has been set free from sin. Now if we have died with Christ, we believe that we will also live with Him. We know that Christ, being raised from the dead, will never die again; death no longer has dominion over Him. For the death He died He died to sin, once for all, but the life He lives He lives to God. So you also must consider yourselves dead to sin and alive to God in Christ Jesus. (Romans 6:3–11)

That old sinful self was taken to the cross and crucified. You are united with Jesus in your Baptism. You are not a slave; God has called you friend. That is your central identity. And this world longs for more people who are part of a Kingdom that is right now and still to come, when there will be no more tears, no more sorrow, no more death. It is groaning with anticipation as it sees more people who have died with Christ. Why? Because it signals that God has not forgotten. He did not look down on His broken creation and throw it away. He redeemed it. Christians, in their baptismal identity, are living proof that God has worked to resurrect that which He created. We are the firstfruits of the new creation, not yet perfected, but a reflection of the Kingdom that is coming.

Jesus has claimed you. There was nothing you could do. He sent the Holy Spirit to bring you into the family. Our identity as children of God is not of our own doing. Even as creation groans for us, it is not because of us. It is because of whose we are.

Discipleship will be a long path. When Jesus issues the Great Commission to "go . . . and make disciples of all nations, baptizing them in the name of the Father and of the Son and of the Holy Spirit, teaching them to observe all that I have commanded you," He is calling His people to a new way (Matthew 28:19–20). He is telling us that as we go, no matter where we are, we are to live as people of the Kingdom. He promises, "I am with you always, to the end of the age." He does not abandon us even as He calls us. The Great Commission does not have an expiration date. When we are brought into the family of God, it becomes part of who we are. It is a lifelong pursuit. He has given us a new identity that is solely based in Him.

Even as we live in that identity, there will still be days when we walk away from it. We are no longer slaves to sin, but sin will constantly seek to re-enslave us. All around us will be whispered lies and temptations, the voice telling us that our new identity in Christ is not enough, that we are not enough, that Jesus is not enough. Sometimes we will believe it. We will lose sight of whose we are. It will lead to selfish ambition and heartache. But our new identity can withstand the attacks of the devil.

When we wander off the path and away from our identity, Jesus brings us back with His good gifts. His Word speaks into our lives, delivering the Holy Spirit to us. That same Spirit brings us back to the Sacraments for renewal. He works through our brothers and sisters in Christ so that we do not walk this path alone. This is our birthright through Baptism. God gives us the wealth of His entire kingdom, purchased with the blood of Jesus on the cross. Yearning to once again return to Jesus, we know that death has no power, just sorrow for a short time. But as we look out into creation, we see the needs that God has placed before us.

Our new identity longs for the new creation. In death, we join with Jesus and the saints before, resting and waiting for the new heavens and new earth. Why, then, are we not snatched away as soon as we join the family? God lets us remain for our neighbors. His love for the world is what keeps us here, even as we know there is something greater to come, as Paul says:

> For to me to live is Christ, and to die is gain. If I am to live in the flesh, that means fruitful labor for me. Yet which I shall choose I cannot tell. I am hard pressed between the two. My desire is to de-

> part and be with Christ, for that is far better. But
> to remain in the flesh is more necessary on your
> account. (Philippians 1:21–24)

Walking the path of discipleship through this world, we learn that the purpose of God for our journey is clear: love God and love our neighbor. It is for their benefit that we remain. Discipleship is rooted in our baptismal identity, so we trust the promises of Jesus and seek to follow Him every day. We look outside of ourselves to our Savior, who is our hope, to encourage the saints and declare the promises of Jesus in the world. Along the way, we continue to find more of ourselves; more of that baptismal identity is revealed, and it is good.

This new identity gives us freedom. We have opportunities to live it out wherever we go, and in so doing, we bring others along for the journey. Look at how Jesus discipled people during His ministry. He gave them the knowledge they would need. Crowds gathered to hear His teaching. Wherever He went, He shared insight into what the kingdom of God looks like and how it should manifest in the world. He quoted the Scriptures and taught from them. Teaching was a key aspect of His ministry—giving knowledge of the ways of God.

Those teachings were not just lectures. Jesus connected to the hearts of people. Standing in front of crowds, He had compassion and connected His teachings to everyday life. His teachings were not some far-off notions of God. Connecting to the hearts of the people around Him, Jesus gave them insight into how their lives mattered to God. These words made faith alive.

Jesus did the work God had sent Him to do. He performed miracles around the countryside, loved the poor and downtrodden, shook up the comfortable religious leaders, and forgave sins. None of that compared to the ultimate act God had sent Him to complete. Jesus went willingly to the cross. Knowing what it meant, knowing the excruciating pain He would experience physically and the utter loneliness He would feel as He uttered the words "My God, My God, why have You forsaken Me?" (Matthew 27:46; Mark 15:34), Jesus went to the cross. He did what God called Him to do. He paid the price that we could not pay.

Then in victory He rose, the joy of Easter morning sending shock waves throughout the world, throughout history. Death was defeated. The women ran to tell the disciples, who hid in fear. But Jesus did what He always does. He came to them. Through locked doors and on the open road, He sought them out. He showed them His hands and feet, proving what He had done. The sacrifice was complete, but it was not one of sorrow. It was a sacrifice of joy. He spent time with His disciples and then once again returned to His Father.

When He did leave, something amazing happened. He worked another miracle. Those apostles who had been closest to Him and the disciples who had followed Him began to take His message to the world. They had experienced Jesus' teaching firsthand. Lives had been changed in front of their eyes while Jesus walked among them. Following Him had been easy because they could see and touch Him daily. But God gave them a gift, the Holy Spirit. With that blessing, they began to spread. Just as their Savior had promised, they were His "witnesses in Jerusalem and in all Judea and Samaria, and to the end of the earth" (Acts 1:8). They took His message wherever they went, seeking to live as He had called them to, loving God and their neighbor.

The first generation of disciples pushed into all corners of the world. With the protected roads of the Roman Empire, they made their way through the Mediterranean lands, some pushing even farther east and south. Churches were established as they went. These churches were not without their problems, but those people lived in their identities and were Kingdom messengers too. They trusted the promises of Jesus and sought to follow Him. Listening to and observing the first generation of disciples, the people of these churches continued the family tradition and made disciples themselves. They multiplied and continued to be living examples of the Kingdom wherever they went.

Nothing could stop them. Paul took the message of Jesus not just to the Jewish people of every town but also to the Gentiles. Through this, God began fulfilling His promise not just to redeem a people but also to save the world. Their message remained the same: Jesus is Lord. They took it in front of crowds, magistrates, and emperors, always seeking the Holy Spirit to speak through them. Some were imprisoned and martyred. But through it all, the Church grew. The kingdom of God was coming near.

Looking at these examples of the faith, we can gain insight into two truths about discipleship.

First, discipleship is about real-life reproduction. Jesus didn't just sit His followers down in a classroom and tell them what it meant to be His disciples. There wasn't a written test. He just said, "Come follow Me." He invited them into His life. There was teaching. Knowledge was an important part of their lives as they followed. But Jesus showed them the way. He taught and then put His teachings into action in front of the disciples. In fact, they often failed at trying to do what Jesus did, and then He had to correct them.

Just reading a book on discipleship is not the whole process. Even adding a discussion group or Bible study around the topic doesn't cover the entire topic. Discipleship is about living life together. It is about encouraging others to see your life and how you trust, seek, and follow Jesus. Paul said it like this: "Be imitators of me, as I am of Christ" (1 Corinthians 11:1). Do not ask people to follow you. Instead, point them to the ways of Christ. Invite them into your life to see how trusting, seeking, and following Him has connected your head, heart, and hands. Continue to be an example in one way that Jesus did not need to be: lead with repentance. Model for others the importance of repenting for sin.

Second, discipleship grows in the soil where it is planted. The churches of Acts looked different from one another. Just look at the letters Paul wrote that are now part of the Bible. While each church had that universal truth—sinners in need of a Savior—each church also had its own unique joys and struggles. Corinth was different from Rome was different from Philippi was different from Ephesus . . . the list goes on. This demonstrates that as disciples brought the message of Jesus and other disciples grew in those places, they each held tightly to the same message while connecting and communicating that message in different ways. Context was important. Disciples in local areas took the message of Jesus and applied it to their lives.

They didn't change the message, but they did bring it to where they were, in the best way possible. Even the creation of elders was a contextual innovation to help the Church:

> In these days when the disciples were increasing in number, a complaint by the Hellenists arose against the Hebrews because their widows were being neglected in the daily distribution. And the twelve summoned the full number of the disciples and said, "It is not right that we should give up preaching the word of God to serve tables. Therefore, brothers, pick out from among you seven men of good repute, full of the Spirit and of wisdom, whom we will appoint to this duty. But we will devote ourselves to prayer and to the ministry of the word." And what they said pleased the whole gathering, and they chose Stephen, a man full of faith and of the Holy Spirit, and Philip, and Prochorus, and Nicanor, and Timon, and Parmenas, and Nicolaus, a proselyte of Antioch. These they set before the apostles, and they prayed and laid their hands on them. And the word of God continued to increase, and the number of the disciples multiplied greatly in Jerusalem. (Acts 6:1–7)

There was a need, they saw it, and they created elders to take care of it. Disciples do not compromise the message, but they look around and grow in the soil in which they are planted. Taking care of the needs around them in new and different ways does not negate the Gospel message. In fact, it is a reflection of the Creator. As image bearers of God, humans create. What better way to create than in the service of God and others?

Here's a question to ask yourself: whom can you invite into your discipleship journey? Look for people ahead of and behind you on the path. Are there those who have more experience than you from whom you want to learn and grow? Is there someone whose faith you want to imitate? Those are the people of faith who can disciple you. They can teach you the ways that God has worked in their lives, how they experience His grace, and how they are following Jesus.

Do not forget about the people behind you. It can be easy to get so caught up in where you are headed and the view where you are that you forget part of being a disciple: discipling others. Whom could you invite to join you along the journey? This isn't about being the greatest scholar or Mother Teresa. It is about encouraging people to take the next step—to trust God, to seek after Him, to follow Jesus where He is leading. Is there someone you can invite to read through this book with you? (I mean, you are almost done; you'd just have to get them to read it!) Are there people who, as Jesus said, are sons and daughters of peace in your life whom you are being called to invite? If you have children, don't forget about them! How are you inviting them into trusting, seeking, and following today? Whether it is one person or a full group, disciples encourage and walk alongside other disciples.

Let people see your daily life following Jesus. Invite them to sit with you in worship and at Bible study. Have them over for dinner. Go out to dinner. Bring them along as you pick up the kids from school or go grocery shopping. Show them what a life of discipleship looks like in the mundane and boring things. Let them see how you trust the promises of Jesus in your life. Give them a taste of what it means to live in your baptismal identity. Share with them the stories of how you have seen God's Word active in your life. Let that be your act of defiance against the enemy, your testimony of how the blood of the Lamb is working in your life. Ask them to serve alongside you. Find opportunities to love your neighbors together.

You are not perfect, but you can serve as an example. Not because of how good you are but because people glimpse the Kingdom through you. This is game tape for them. They are watching the footage of your life as you trust, seek, and follow. Because of the invitation, they will get to see faith lived out in daily life. Discipleship is not some pie-in-the-sky theory. No, this is the journey through the everyday things.

Work to be willing to show them some of the unpleasant times too. Don't just put on a happy-go-lucky veneer. Let them see what happens when you fail. This is not to pull you down but instead to show the rhythm of life as a disciple, a life not of perfection but of love and repentance. A life that returns over and again, through confession and absolution, to the deep well of the Gospel. A life centered on Jesus and His promises. Grow in the soil where you are planted. Look for opportunities around you. Don't be jealous of where others are, and don't remain stagnant. Instead, root deeply in the promises of Jesus and look at what God has placed in front of you.

This is a simple process. There is not some grand formula, and the way the journey works with one person may look different with the next person. This journey is about returning to trusting the promises of Jesus and seeking to follow Him. It can be done by CEOs, farmers, teachers, pastors, students, mothers—the list does not end. Jesus did not set up complex hoops for you to jump through to be His disciple. You are made a disciple in the waters of Baptism. Walking on the journey is a part of the process of sanctification, re-creation, in your life.

Discipleship is not only for "super Christians." It is for everyday people. "You can't be a disciple; you're not _____." Fill in the blank with how it has appeared to you. This is a lie of the enemy, not the truth of Jesus. The truth is we are all just at different places on the path. Any system of discipleship that sets up rankings or value of one over another does not recognize the beauty that discipleship is for all baptized believers. It is part of our inheritance as members of the family of God.

If the way ever seems overwhelming or too complicated, stop and take a rest. Resting is not bad. In fact, God gifts us with a full day of it every week! It is so important to Him that He commands it! You should be taking time to simply sit down and rest in the promises of Jesus. Discipleship is about bearing the fruit that God has blessed us with. When it seems as if we are not bearing fruit or some of that fruit has turned sour, it is time to rest. Abide in Jesus, and remember these words:

> I am the true vine, and My Father is the vinedresser. Every branch in Me that does not bear fruit He takes away, and every branch that does bear fruit He prunes, that it may bear more fruit. Already you are clean because of the word that I have spoken to you. Abide in Me, and I in you. As the branch cannot bear fruit by itself, unless it abides in the vine, neither can you, unless you abide in Me. I am the vine; you are the branches. Whoever abides in Me and I in him, he it is that bears much

fruit, for apart from Me you can do nothing. If anyone does not abide in Me he is thrown away like a branch and withers; and the branches are gathered, thrown into the fire, and burned. If you abide in Me, and My words abide in you, ask whatever you wish, and it will be done for you. By this My Father is glorified, that you bear much fruit and so prove to be My disciples. As the Father has loved Me, so have I loved you. Abide in My love. (John 15:1–9)

Resting and abiding in Jesus is essential on this journey. He will work to remove the excess weight that burdens you. He will cut off that which is not bearing fruit and destroy it. Even vines go through dormant times throughout the year. It is not a constant harvest. There are times of rest. As a disciple, you will need these times. Time to slow down and catch your breath. Time to reevaluate and pray, asking the Lord to reveal to you the places that are bearing fruit and those that are not. Time to pray and ask to see the lies you might be believing, whispered words that are piling guilt and shame onto your shoulders instead of freedom. Only in rest can you take the time to see these things. They are the enemy's way of pulling you off the path with burdens.

Discipleship is not about tests you need to pass. It is not a classroom in which you memorize all the ways of God. Nor is it a measuring cup to be filled with all your good works so that one day you may finally please God. It is a journey, a long path in the direction of the kingdom of God. It will be full of stops and starts, hiccups and confusion. But it will be the greatest joy of your life.

Discipleship is anchored by the promises of Jesus. Through Jesus, you are bought at a price; that love is inescapable. He became a man to go to the cross, for you. That's the power for the journey of discipleship: Jesus for us. His promises are good and true. Trusting them gives us salvation and hope, which fuels us for a life of discipleship. Do not look to your works for this hope. They will fail you. Do not look to other people for this steadfast love. They will fail you. But Jesus' promise remains. It holds steadfast when everything else slips away.

Seek God and hear His voice in your life. There is nothing mystical here. Open the Word of God. Keep your Bible close at hand. Read His Word and see how it interacts with your life. It is not dead words on a page. No, it is the voice of God boldly proclaiming His love for you and the way in which you should go. It is a simple but profound gift that enables you to connect to God every day. Be in prayer. Constantly. Let that be a driving force as you seek God. It will change your heart even as you bring your petitions before Him. As you seek Him, watch how it turns to following, how seeking and praying are beautifully woven together with following your Savior.

Follow Jesus in your life. He has you where He needs you. Ask Him what He is calling you to do in those places. Be a storyteller of the Kingdom with your words and actions. Wherever you go, follow Him and "proclaim the excellencies of Him who called you out of darkness into His marvelous light" (1 Peter 2:9).

It is a simple way. Trusting, seeking, and following. The journey will bring you to the highest mountaintops and through the lowest valleys. Jesus will always be with you. It is His promise. While it may be difficult, it is not complicated. It is not a five-step solution—"If only you do these things well you will have reached your destination." In fact, it is not a destination. This journey is a longing for the Kingdom that will reach its fullness when Jesus comes again. It is a gift of being a part of the Kingdom here on earth.

Continue this journey today. As your feet hit the floor, pray a simple prayer: "May trusting in Your promises be my foundation. May Your Word come alive as I seek You. May I see where You have called me to follow You today." Then start getting ready for your day. Now repeat that for the rest of your life. But simple does not mean boring. While it may be simple, this journey will be the greatest you could ever undertake. At your Baptism, Jesus placed your feet on the path. He invited you: "Come, follow Me." Share the journey in community. Let the blessings of the Lord be not just your own but also shared together with the Body of Christ. May those brothers and sisters encourage and challenge you, as you do the same for them.

There will be days that are full of joy. Trust, seek, follow.

There will be days when all that can be found is sorrow. Trust, seek, follow.

When the way is clear or clouded. When you feel ready to go or sluggish to move forward. When you are surrounded by friends or feeling lonely.

Trust. Seek. Follow.

In those simple things, watch what our God can do, and be amazed.

DISCIPLESHIP COMMUNITY

OPEN WITH PRAYER

Ask for a volunteer to open with prayer. Rotate who does this each time you get together. Praying in front of people may scare you, but it is worth growing in the practice. Praying together is part of what the Body of Christ does. Not only is it our connection to God but it also gives an example of how we live on this discipleship journey.

FROM LAST TIME

How's your next step going?

DISCUSSION

1. What jumped out to you in this chapter?

2. How does your mind-set shift when you realize you have a new baptismal identity? Or how does it refocus you if it was just a reminder?

3. Name someone who is discipling you. Who is someone you could be discipling?

4. How does discipleship happen in your daily life?

DO IT

Keep meeting. Discipleship doesn't happen only when this book is open. Keep walking through the three questions together. Worship together. Pray together. Love your neighbors together. This book is built as a launch pad, not a finish line.

Commit to getting together for the next six months to a year. Find Scriptures to walk through together and work through the three questions. Share your testimony. Tell the story of Jesus!

THE THREE QUESTIONS

Choose your own adventure! What have you been reading lately in Scripture? Apply the three questions to that!

1. What is God saying?

2. What is He calling me to do?

3. What is my next step?

CLOSING

Make sure you know when you are getting together next.

Pray for one another. Take prayer requests and close in prayer. Spread out the prayer requests so as many people are praying as are available.